A POETRY ODYSSEY

A COLLECTION OF VERSE

EDITED BY DAISY JOB

First published in Great Britain in 2021 by:

Young Writers
Remus House
Coltsfoot Drive
Peterborough
PE2 9BF
Telephone: 01733 890066
Website: www.youngwriters.co.uk

Book Design by Ashley Janson

Softback ISBN 978-1-80015-120-8

Printed and bound in the UK by BookPrintingUK
Website: www.bookprintinguk.com
YB0453C

FOREWORD

Welcome, Reader, to
A Poetry Odyssey - A Collection Of Verse.

We at Young Writers are proud to present this collection of poetry exhibiting creations from children aged 5 to 18 that cover a wind range of topics. You will be reading poems dedicated to and celebrating loved ones, poems inspired by nature and what we need to do to protect it, and poems about today's issues and how they wish to change things.

Here at Young Writers it is our aim to instil a love of poetry and nurture the creative talents of the next generation. We hope to build confidence in expressing themselves through poetry and this anthology gives them the opportunity to express themselves in any way the children choose. Having their poem in print will hopefully carry that confidence on and will serve as a lifelong reminder of their skill and creativity.

It never ceases to fascinate us what the latest generation choose to write about in their poetry because if their poetry reflects the society they will build and the creative projects they will go on to produce, then we're looking forward to the future.

CONTENTS

THE POEMS

Featherby Values

Like our sister and brother before us, into a school we were thrust,
Our parents put us into Featherby, a name that they can trust.
There's Mr Ballard and Mr Thomas, who is quite witty,
Then there's Mr Brenton, who teaches us unity.
When we go to the school gate, each morning he will patiently wait.
It's Milo, our new Head, who always listens to what we've read.
Why is Miss Massey not with Milo?
Of course, Miss Massey is dreaming of sun, sea and a lilo.
Who is that dreaming of being the next X Factor star?
It's Mr Bryden, with his guitar.
It's the teachers who set the pace,
But is it Miss Hopkins or Miss Witt who will win the race?
Who is that getting Mr Graham to run faster?
Why it's Miss McMaster.
The schoolwork is not what we would expect,
Without this, we would not learn respect.
During this pandemic, the world has sat on the fence,
We are the children of Featherby, and we have resilience.
If you want to choose a school, where the teachers are cool.
Then choose Fearherby, where you learn responsibility,
Most importantly, you will learn about loyalty and honesty.

Isaac, Mason & Beau Godden (11)

The Clock

The clock,
It gives you the pressure of its ticking,
Suppressing any good or bad emotion.
All that's left is the perplexity of this substantial world.
It looks you right in the eye,
You try to keep calm,
But the ticking gets on the nerves.
The prefrontal cortex is extinguished,
As all that is left of the neurons is the insula.
But soon that will break down,
Any kind of happiness breaks now.
You feel the clock tick in an eerie way.
It's like a bomb's ticking.
It takes your breath away.
You feel suffocated.
But with no doubt, you run away,
Rapidly, strongly, until you fall down.
You freeze.
You fall unconscious.
When you wake up, broken bits of the room of isolation lies
on the ground.
Your head hurts,
You're confused.
Was your curiosity that contagious everything in the room
broke down to bits?
You shudder to think.

There's dust scattered everywhere.
There's no time to stay.
You pick yourself up and try to call the police,
But you remember you are in isolation with no cell phone.
But then your doubts come in,
Maybe you're daydreaming?
Maybe it's just a nightmare?
No one can tell the answer.
You remember that you were in a room of isolation before,
Nobody to call.
You don't have your cell phone with you.
You're stuck.
All alone.
Afraid, that there's something.
Something coming for you.
You think that all hope is lost
Because
You try every possible way.
But resilience isn't enough for the world to have faith in you.
You parents never told you your status on religion.
You don't know if you believe in God.
So praying to no one did no good. The world revolves around you.
Your eye cracks a tear.
Deep inside you know that you're in danger.
The damaged door creaks slightly.
You turn around slowly.

You hide in a corner and close your eyes.
Then you open them and
A black, indistinct and dark figure knocks you out.
Next thing you know,
You're in hospital as soon as you open your eyes.
Your parents are there, bursting out into tears.
Your sister looks frightened.
Your family members all look like they're full of grief.
Then the doctor appears saying unbelievable words out of his mouth
And then everyone falls silent.
The doctor turns around to tell you what has made everyone quiet.
The doctor looks at you.
He sits down and says to listen very carefully.
He says your life is in danger.
He looks down and says that it isn't a contagious disease or issue but,
He says
You have cancer.
You shout loudly.
The doctor tells you to calm down.
He says it can be cured
Because it's only the first stage.
You say, at least some good relief.
But it's still cancer, he says gloomily.
You look down and a tear drops down.

You gulp.
Your sister hugs you tightly,
Same as your mum and dad.
You sigh with grief.
The clock is a contagious disease.
Its ticking struck you, you think.
The clock has a mind of its own.

Eesha Nair (10)

Living With Anxiety

Living with anxiety you are trapped in your own body.
It's something that starts small and gradually takes over your life.
It's an illness you can't see or people can't know about because it's a
Hidden one, it's a mental one.
It's not a nice one, you wake up and don't want to face the day.
You lie in bed crying silently to yourself, wishing the pain would go away.
But you wipe away the tears and draw a smile on your face as if nothing has happened.
You go to school and people are laughing so loud it feels like your head's going to pop
And footsteps feel like an earthquake but it's really not that noisy but to you it is.
You see a teacher you say hi to and smile
But inside you're crying, hearing what's your own voice,
But really your anxiety is saying how fat, ugly and worthless you are.
You're turning on yourself and you don't even know it.
You don't tell anyone but try and face the day you dread.
You sit there silently to yourself.
Well, it feels like that but you're surrounded with people,
Too many, it feels like there's no air in the room.
They're in your face, go away, no, I can't,

But really they're all doing their own thing.
And you ask to go to the toilet and cry,
Cry because it's all too much, how you wish it would all stop and go away.
You wipe away the tears and go in as if nothing has happened
But then it's all too much, this time you get up and go and never go back.
You sit there reflecting on it,
Knowing what you have just done but realising what's just happened and you say, "No, no, no, what have you done?" sobbing to yourself.
You're scared and hot and sweaty, there's no air to breathe.
I can't breathe.
Your bloodshot eyes, you don't trust anyone they might hurt you.
All these thoughts swirling around in your head, not knowing what to think.
No, no, please stop and you finally go and find someone who you trust a bit.
They can see your distress, they feel it.
They try and reassure you. "Don't touch me," you're saying to yourself.
But you're scared, you flinch, your body moves for you.
They're away from you but it feels as if they're in your face,
As if they're going to hurt you but all they want to do is help.
You cry and wish it all away but it won't.

You've just got to live with it as best you can.
You don't want to be like this not going out when your friends ask.
You are too scared to leave your own house.
You want to be happy and live your life but it's hard,
But this isn't you, this is your anxiety.

Aleece Jones (16)

Corona

Corona, Corona, I can't stand the name,
You came and caused so much pain.
The poor NHS working so hard,
All you do is come and try and take charge.
Everyone will remember the year 2020,
When Corona came and destroyed so many.
The teachers still teaching,
And all the key workers we owe so much.
To all the people that have died from this virus,
And the loved ones you wish you could give them one last kiss.
You came and spread your virus across the nation,
You weren't even given an invitation.
But we are strong, and we will fight
To get this virus out of our lives.
So, for now, we need to stay at home to save precious lives,
While the NHS risk everything in their fight to defeat COVID-19.
The nation has come together in strange and uncertain times,
But we will see our families and friends soon.
Our lives will eventually go back to normal,
While Corona will hopefully be sent on its way.
So thank you, everyone, who does so much to keep us safe,
So we can return to a safer place.

Sienna Elizabeth Borges (10)

As The World Comes To A Halt

There is finally time now for everyone
to 'stand and stare' as WH Davies put it just over a century ago,
'What is this life if, full of care
We have no time to stand and stare
No time to see the woods we pass,
Where squirrels hide their nuts in grass...

Life seemed busy with people working long hours
The economy in full swing
Children used to daily routines at home and school
Most people were planning their next holiday
As summer is the time to enjoy the weather
But the whole world came to a standstill
As COVID-19 appears from nowhere
And spreads all around the world

There is panic buying
There is sickness
There is death
COVID-19 stopped the world in its tracks
Leaving people unable to do their regular tasks
We are told to wash our hands
Use face masks
Practise social distancing

Streets are deserted
No longer meeting family and friends
Unable to do much except stand and stare from balconies and windows
As this is the only option to have a glimpse of the outside world
Parks and playgrounds near but deserted
As scientists identify the dangers of sharing
There is nowhere to go
There is no one to see
Travellers stranded in different countries around the world
Some on holiday, some away on business, some gone to work
Away from their family and friends
They are scared
Yearning to return to their homeland

But this temporary slowdown of human activity has had a profound impact on many species
With fewer people in urban environments,
Much less traffic on the roads and noise pollution at its lowest
Some species are making the most of their time
Wild animals are turning up in places they have not been seen in decades

COVID-19 is a virus impossible to see with naked eyes
But it seems that it is nature's weapon in the fight against humanity

With hidden benefits, the lockdown has made the world realise that nature has so much to offer
As we look at the shapes of the cloud
we see pigeons walking in a group like family,
We can hear sweet birdsongs early in the morning
And notice how trees wave to us in the gentle breeze

Many of us are getting inspired by the beauty of nature;
Come walk with me into the forest's blessed abode
To see the wondrous beauty the Earth has bestowed upon us
We shall bask in the surreal splendour that surrounds us
And listen to nature orchestrating the forest's magnum opus.

Sonakshi Devi Seetohul

Kashmir

In between India and Pakistan lies the Kashmiri land
Where all sorts of things have been outlawed and banned.

The WiFi and signal are in lockdown
And to remain safe you need to keep down

All town squares have become an empty space
As the law says, 'no more than four people meeting in one place'.

The reason for all these bothersome effects
Are two countries that are at each other's necks
Fighting over by whom Kashmir should be run
Both countries claiming that they are 'the one'.

Hindus take the claim as Kashmir's leader is one of them
He says, "Only Hindus can sort out this mayhem!"

The Muslims complain, "Hey, save that for later!
Muslim population here is shown to be much greater!"

As the quarrel gets even more serious, new problems have begun to arise
Such as great, big bombs exploding from the skies
And revolts being held throughout the cities
Demanding the country should change its committees.

With all this happening, Kashmir doesn't know what to do!
They just want to know who is being ruled by who!

Lily Gould (11)

House On Fire

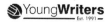

What lays before our eyes,
no one can really tell,
the secrets of one's life,
let's move to someone else,
ask the man on the moon,
he'll say a house on fire,
what he can see from his view,
you'll laugh and say look higher,
we don't want this,
we want to resist,
we need to resist,
what was discovered in 1862,
President Trump still thinks is a hoax,
it shocks us all and seems so new,
but I promise you, it's not a joke,
we can work through this,
together we will end this,
the act of using CO2 we slaughter,
but still have no reasons for hurricanes,
but act surprised when there's a rise in water,
but still have no reason for the sudden pains,
how can we look forward to a future?
How can we think about what we want,
if we won't live to see it?
Let's talk about the future; specifically 2045,

28,000 wildlife species will become extinct,
will it even fully survive,
if we keep burning down the places in which they live?
We're mad at others,
but we are the monsters,
we are the killers,
and what happened to the North Pole,
our ice caps have completely melted into water,
have we finally reached our goal,
for it does exist no longer,
we're killing the world we live in,
all for nothing,
oh well,
how about the pollution caused by plastic,
every year eight million tons escape into the oceans,
the cause of all the statics,
forming a deadly, toxic potion,
no one cares,
all we care about is what we want,
I want money,
I want success,
2050; our future has been stolen,
everyone is left lying weak,
for nothing richer than gold and,
lives have been stolen but we're the thieves,
we're the bad guys,
we set our house on fire,

ask the people who have lost their homes,
after they finish crying,
they'll tell you all you need to know,
they'll tell you all about it,
but don't ask,
they don't want to talk about it,
close your eyes and imagine a breathing earth,
now open and compare,
for the last time; global warming is a real issue,
now you know please share,
what lays before our eyes,
no one can really tell,
the secrets of one's life,
let's move to someone else.

Saron Ghebremeskel (14)

My Mother Is A Tree

My heart stood still when you went away,
I loved you every moment, every second, every day.

And though I'm trying hard to move on,
I still can't shake the fact you're gone.

"Where could you be?" I cry, "Please, Mother, I'm all by myself."
Then I see a stack of photos sitting on the shelf.

I grip onto a photo, tracing my fingertips over your face,
Memories flood back, have I finally cracked this case?

I doubt myself but recall your wise words,
"Enriched in soil, beleaguered by birds."

I grin in triumph, I'm now aware,
I have fulfilled the void that has always been there.

I look out the window and watch the sun go down,
The trees stand tall, yet their leaves turn brown.

I stumble across the tree of heaven, connecting your roots to my every bone,
I place my hand on Mother Nature and instantly know it's this tree that you own.

I cry in alleviation, past the darkness, I can finally see,
It's what you chose to pursue after death, my mother is a tree.

Lola Piric (15)

Heroes

Are you alarmed yet?
They say this thing, it
Kills your immune system,
silent but violent,
Attacks your lungs
Makes it
difficult to breathe
And it's spreading...
Spreading like wildfire
Causing havoc
Your friends and family
May catch it,
If they don't
Already have it
It's tragic I tell you,
Madness
Scientists say
Old people get it worse
But most
Get it after a phase of time
It doesn't choose specifically,
It's wild
It affects
The rich, poor, young, old
The unknown, the famous

It's vicious
Everyone's on edge
Locked inside of their homes
Nervously
Borders are closed
Countries declare
State of emergencies
Grocery stores are cleared
Nobody's praying in places of worship
The world
Has
Us
In
lockdown
No wonder toilet paper
Sold out first
The stock market crashed,
Dramatically,
Thousands laid off work
Hand sanitizer is going for
A million pounds a squirt
You better not sneeze because
No one's gonna say
God bless you
They might even arrest you
I don't mean to stress you
But washing your hands obsessively

In the restroom will not protect you
Listen to me
Like every tragedy
We can let this
Destroy us
Or we can use it
To our absolute benefit
And repair relationships and counsel
Its time we take our civic role,
And plant a hole
of our biggest weakness
Have you ever heard of a hero...?
A hero with no cape?
But helps show the fire escape
To freedom
Not fazed by a single thing
Well those people are key workers
Working their lives off
Like case workers
The only vaccine for this pandemic is,
To stimulate our heroes,
This nation needs to solute the heroes,
Of our marvel universe,
as without them our life would be zero,
And that's why I choose YOU as my hero.

Yameen Rahman (12)

When The World Was On Pause

Before the world was on pause, people walked the streets,
Children played in the park with their friends, feeling complete,
There was a rumour of a monster, slender and quick,
That rode from person to person and killed with a click,
But it would never reach us, the politicians and newsreaders said,
Little did they know, this monster was mankind's biggest threat,
Days and weeks went by and it had finally arrived,
The government had been blind,
Because in truth, they had lied,
They had joked about its presence,
But the monster was spreading, it was seeding its incurable essence,
They tried to stop it with all of their might,
And the public thought there was hope and there had to be light,
When the world was on pause, the streets were silent,
Children were inside alone, and hushed to be compliant,
Parliament sat collectively in guilt,
They had no cure for the monster, it was a tree that could not wilt.

Jake Bridges

Children's Feelings

One day we had everyone around us to laugh and joke
Then the next we had a storm that blew us all away
Away in our homes.

We had a sudden shock, we had nowhere to go
We were all stuck at home, no school, no outings
A big virus landed on our planet
Coronavirus, deadly taking over our lives.

My dad has no work, my mum keeps on working for the NHS
Looking after those vulnerable families in need
Keep up your good work Mum!

We washed our hands so often to protect ourselves
And others around us
We found we are now experts at washing our hands.

Every day we clean and disinfect to wipe all the germs
The bleach and Dettol working together to sparkle.

We wake every day and have so much to keep us entertained
We do lots of reading, listening, we keep our minds active with our educational activities.
We have a break and play on our PlayStation.

Despite having fun at home
We are still alone,
We miss our friends and family

(Can't wait to reach out to them once the crisis is over and out)
The streets calm and bare
The sun is shining bright
Virus is stopping us from going out
Every corner you turn, every hour we watch go by
We pray all the people that have been affected recover
We pray that everything will wipe the virus away
Far, far away, never to be seen again.

Once we have combatted the virus with a fight
We will survive and come back
Clean surfaces, clean streets, cautious about touching things.

Once again we meet again and are able to meet our friends and family
Have a laugh, joke and smile
Play in the parks in the beautiful weather
So, for now, hold up strong, we are all in this together
Time is a healer,
Time will tell if we stick indoors
Won't be for long if we follow the Government's Guidelines
Pray for everyone and stay safe at all time
We can get through this difficult time.

Abdul-Rafay Bilal

Lady Winter

There she is, outside
enticing you to come and join in on the fun.
She shows you the carpets of white snow,
shimmering on the hills.
The crisp carpet underneath your feet,
muffles your footsteps.
As the savage, bone-crushing cold
like the jacks of a vice,
clamps you within its chilling claws.

She shows you her frost-covered Winter Wonderland,
with bitter winds and trees like ice sculptures.
Frost glitters; a diamond necklace.
Icicles hang down from trees like earrings,
Delicately and beautifully.

She wants you to forget the sunshine,
and delight in her white, whirling world of snowflakes.
For the ferocity of the cold to take your breath away.
For there not to be a horizon.
In her white world, still, silent and eerie.
She wants a billowing, white ocean blending into the sky.
She wants the snow, too heavy for the branches,
to fall in a delicate shower over our head.

Cloaked in dazzling snow,
a bitter whirl of ice crystals,

swirls about Lady Winter,
as she moves silently; a spectre, through her world of white.
She's albino-faced,
with a dress made from pristine, icy snowflakes,
gliding through her white world.

She says goodbye to you.
She knows her reign is coming to an end...
Gracefully, she meets Sir Spring,
bestows him her majestic crown.

She looks at you and says,
"It's goodbye for now.
However, soon I shall restore my crown."

Mesmerising, she turns her piercing eyes of icy blue towards you,
deep pools of power,
"Remember me!"
A request or a warning?
I feel a shiver up my spine,
as she melts away,
relaxing her icy grip on my heart.

Rahul Thapar

A Saving Grace

2020 has been a bad year
It doesn't seem to bring us any cheer
We sleep in the morning and are awake in the night
2020 is going to give us a fright

We are like an apple just rotting away
No person would ever want it that way
We have lost track of time and communication
We are busy making charts and using tabulation

We are all lions living in our den
My lockdown experience, God help me, Amen
With crashing and banging and crying, plus tears
Some parents are drinking lots of gin and beers

Our homes are a prison and I really can't bear
We go to the window and do nothing but stare
With TV, Xbox and phones galore
We couldn't really ask for anything more

But there is still some hope, we've mentioned nothing positive
We need to work together and be more causative
There's family time and playing outside
But remember the rules we need to abide

There's art and cooking and things creative
We can dress up as tribes and can be Native

Don't go out when you're not allowed
Stay home, be safe and make Britain proud

We can watch movies on our comfy seats
And listen to our catchy beats
There's cards and chess and draughts, even Scrabble
We can fight and argue, it's one big rabble

The NHS is doing amazingly well
There are shopkeeps struggling and planning to sell
COVID-19 has a grinning face
We all just need a saving grace.

Cameron Monie (13)

Beyond

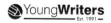

It's not what you feel
It's not how or when you heal
Once you were dancing in your heels
Now you're lying sick like a dead eel
For everyone I have to be strong
Even if it seems wrong... sometimes
I don't know what you have done to deserve this
You shouldn't be going through this
Why did God do this?

Just why?

Your presence
Vibe
Sensitivity
Strength
Determination
Warmth
And many more

Parts of me are gone
What have I done?
Didn't even get to say one
Single word to you 'cause you're gone

Can't look at anything good without pouring out a whole ocean
You left your mark on me, a deep one

Hurts so much I can't get any sleep
The darkness now creeps its way into all my parts, entering every blood vessel
The murderer that took you away from me is still out there
It's in the air, catching millions of victims each second
You were the shield that kept them all away
My shield got shattered into pieces in a battle that wasn't even ours

Can't eat
Sleep
Think
Or do anything without feeling emptiness

Parts of me are gone
What have I done?
Didn't even get to say one
Single word to you 'cause you're gone

Maybe I'll see you again
Maybe I won't see you again

Only God knows.

Suunga Mungwala (16)

Exceptional Being

Have you ever seen a light in human form?
Whenever they're around, you feel loved and warm,
They radiate serenity and hope,
Without them, you don't know how you would cope.

My mum is all this and more,
If there was a chart for the best, she would definitely have the highest score.
She is adored by all,
Whenever I need her, I never hesitate to call.

She has taught me how to endure life,
How to be strong and one day be an amazing wife.
She is always there for me,
She can't swim, but if I was drowning in the sea I can guarantee
She would dive in to save me,
A mother's love cannot surpass this, do you agree?

You have sacrificed so much for my brother and I,
I love you and celebrate you, like the 4th of July!
You are my best friend, that I cannot deny.

You motivate me to be successful,
Although there will be challenges,
Although it will be stressful,
I will endeavour to make you proud,
I will remain an individual, I will always stand apart from the crowd.

You hold my heart forever,
You are the world's greatest treasure,
Your beauty is evident,
You have great humour, that is also definitely relevant.

I can never thank you enough,
I know the journey has been rough,
But you were resilient, you remained tough,
To turn around and see your smile, has always been enough.

Rosemary Lawal (17)

The Magic Box

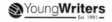

Inspired by 'The Magic Box' by Kit Wright

I will put in the box:
A bright rainbow made with colourful sweet-tasting roses
You can slide down with a big weeee and swoosh
At the end of the smiling slide which goes on and on
You will land in a gigantic candy box which can splat you with joy.

I will put in the box:
All my favourite books which all come amazingly true
Opening these is magical, the colourful characters all fall out
Like Gangsta Granny
Who would come to life
And do some cool stuff but no more stealing
And lots of adventures including scaring the very nosy policeman away.

I will put in the box:
All the delicious and yummy things to eat that you can only imagine
Strawberry and creamy pancakes which are as big as the biggest bear
Bubblegum ice lollies and never-ending bubblegum juice made with the bubbliest bubblegum
You can smell and taste all your imaginary favourite foods.

My box is fashioned from:
Not wooden but sensible and strong seaside rock
With lots of swirly colours, which swirl and swirl into a swirly song and surprise
Covered in seventy-seven stars and sparkles that sparkle super-duper strong and bright
With every touch you make the magic box, superpowers will come into you
And make you smile as bright as the seventy-seven stars again and again
You are flying forever and ever until bedtime comes
And then the magic box and your powers will have a rest
Until it's time and time again to sail and show the magic box and your light to the world again.

Aleesa Afzal (8)

The Grounded Witch

Once a witch you're always a witch,
Or so thought Agnes who one day found herself in a ditch,
You see Agnes was the one that could always fly,
But on this particular day, she fell from the sky,
She brushed herself off and up she got,
With her broom in her hand, she was hot to trot,
She tried and tried with all her heart,
But her broomstick just would not start,
So off she walked to the nearest town,
Determined to turn her frown upside down,
Have you ever heard of a witch that walks!
It's like a seagull that never squawks!
Into town she went with all her might,
But what to do in the middle of the night,
She was hungry and she was scared,
But there were no villagers around! No one cared,
You see Agnes was a wicked witch,
Some would say she deserved that ditch,
Nightfall ended and morning soon came,
Agnes was woken by a strange-looking flame,
Her fire was about to go out,
When a fire pixie gave her a clout,
You see Agnes had taken her favourite spot,
When she laid her head she must have forgotten,
Witches can fly but they need pixie dust,

A fire one that they can trust,
Agnes had never been grounded before,
Out of her context, that's for sure,
The little pixie nice and robust,
Sprinkled Agnes with plenty of dust,
With a kick start her broomstick rose,
And off Agnes flew, away she goes,
You see we are not always what we seem,
Black could be white and yellow could be green...

Daisy Adela Anderson (10)

The Great Dragon Biraile

Over the meadow is a thing we don't speak of,
A thing we don't know,
It is said to be a dragon,
A great mighty one that could kill you with just one talon.
All our noble soldiers and warriors,
Never told us the fable of the great dragon Biraile.
But I ventured out one day,
In the dead of night to meet the great dragon Biraile.
With a sack of supplies,
A stolen sword and a shield,
I knew this could include a pack of old lies.
Over the hill I went,
As fit as a fiddle as brave as a lion.
I looked back at my longing lodging,
As it might be the last time I would be seeing.
I peeped over the hedge expecting to see the great dragon Biraile.
What I saw then,
Possibly couldn't be the great dragon Biraile.
It was a baby dragon,
As small and cute as can be,
No bigger than a miniature wagon.
It took me a moment to realize,
When I plucked up my courage and ventured onwards.
There I saw the most astonishing thing ever
A gargantuan dragon and a hatched egg.

But wait, it was wheezing and gasping,
There and then it collapsed dead.
It's not a usual sight to see a dragon die
Nor what had just happened.
The first prickles of sunlight on the back of my neck,
Told me I ought to dash back.
I grasped the baby dragon and leapt over the hill and into bed.
I shoved the dragon in my cupboard,
And pulled my blanket over my head.
What was my mother to say?

Maneesh Pyati (10)

The Sea

The sea is a noxious giant under the dark abyss
It is conspicuous and indulges anything that it seeks
Ocean and sea higher than the frosty white-coated peaks
They both conspire and besiege the creatures of the deep

In the dull, deep, dusty sea were the alluring creatures
Dishevelled seaweed lay as thin as a twig in dismay
They have to endure the treacherous waves
The colossal breakers crash down without a care
Not all hope is despair

In the interior of the sea lay tears of sorrow
A covert piece of merriment waiting to be dispersed
There lay a heart made of gold and happiness in the vast sea
The creatures have conversed

To help the sea forage for lustre
When the sun has raised
The darkness has diminished and been demolished
And had its day
As all beings in the sea praise
The unangered waves

The sea is docile to everyone
And has a very kind gesture with
All his funny puns

But with every calamity comes a consequence
Now the sea has to tolerate with the aftermath

It was a very long debate
So, the sea had to wait, he wasn't obstinate
The price was extravagant
Finally, they told him he had to be meticulous
From this day forward the sea wasn't conspicuous
They called him the salty sea
He devoted all his candour and time to everyone
And he was never malicious again.

Naiya Patel (10)

Bangladesh

Back home is something special
A memory that cannot be thrown away
But a memory that can be made all over again
A community that is like no other
A life that begins without a starter
This is Bangladesh

Having crops and natural medicine
There are some things that go beyond boundaries
The love that escapes from city to city
Making much from little
Nothing we make is brittle
This is Bangladesh

I remember the sight that both dazzled and scared me
An elephant roaming through the streets of Jessore
I remember feeling free, free from the captivity
A range of excitement found in activities
This is Bangladesh

Following in the footsteps of my ancestors
Following their path to success
This is Bangladesh

A country of traditions
A whole world of politicians
Bangladesh

A country of laughter, songs and colour
This is Bangladesh

I refresh my mind
Putting pen down to paper
A whole new life but without an eraser
A life of hardships
But not for me
This, to you, is Bangladesh

So I start this poem again
Using no fancy words to keeping it simple
Back home is something special
Something special is what takes me there
That special thing is simple: Bangladesh
Bangladesh is where I'm from and
This is Bangladesh.

Eliza Islam

Hugs And Kisses

A tear rolled down my sorrowful face,
As you heard me begin to weep.
You strolled over to me and smiled,
My heart began to leap.
I adore your hugs and kisses,
And how they make me feel.
When I'm feeling wounded,
They help me start to heal.
Do you remember that enjoyable time,
When we went on a tiring walk?
I'll never forget those special moments,
When all we did was talk.
Your eyes are like the sparkling sun,
When it's not hiding behind the pouring rain,
Your hair is soft and silky,
And you have a very clever brain.
When I see a light,
I only think of you,
Your eyes twinkle like a star,
But when you leave me, it breaks my heart in two.
I'll never call you 'Mum',
You'll always be known as Mummy,
You are a very cool person,
And sometimes a little bit funny.
You are as perfect as can be,

Even when you don't try,
Every time I'm with you,
I feel as if I can fly.
No matter how grumpy I am,
You always make my day,
I just want to say that I love you,
In every single way.
I love you, Mummy.

Imogen Grace Thomas-Eardley (11)

My Superhero

I really like superheroes,
They're very super indeed.
They're awesome, hardworking people
Who do their good deeds.

My favourite superhero is Spider-Man.
He can shoot webs everywhere!
He can trap enemies as if they were flies
With the webs stuck to their hair.

His webs could cover a building,
Or just a tiny shoe.
If I put my foot in it,
It would stick forever like glue!

Can he swing off buildings?
Yes, it is very true...
But I'd prefer a different power
Maybe you would, too.

I'd make others go super slow
While I would whizz past!
It's great to be a superhero
If you can go super-fast.

I'll find many people and places
When I whizz around faster and faster,

Wouldn't I be able to spot
And stop awaiting disasters?

A good superhero like Spider-Man
Should be adventurous and bold.
They should also be trustworthy
And not be a villain at all...

Superheroes are busy,
Like bees in a hive.
You can be a superhero
And help them to save lives.

Methu Menuwara (9)

The Change I Want To See

The change I want to see is equal privilege for black people and white people,
Justice is key and for justice black people will fight,
White people have more than enough justice in their lives,
What I pray for is for the races to unite.
As black people we have an expectation,
It's about time we feel some elation,
Protests and thoughts have been spread around the nation,
But still, there is a lot of discrimination.

The change I want to see is for this virus to be eradicated,
For black people COVID-19 is another fight so their lives won't be eliminated,
They are losing hope and good feelings aren't being stimulated,
And this virus is killing thousands and our world is being annihilated.
I know many people are dying,
I know many people are crying,
But we need to keep on trying,
Before, our world becomes terrifying.

The change I want to see is for the human race to unite,
The change I want to see is for this virus to die,

The change I want to see is for everything to be alright,
The change I want to see is for there to be no more fight!

Emmanuel Parry (12)

The Beatles Tribute

In Liverpool, the journey began
Four men, one band
Memories were made
As outstanding songs were played.

Legends will stay with us forever
And will leave us never
Those four will stay in our hearts
Along with their beautiful art.

John Lennon was the main
Paul McCartney had the fame
George Harrison made them strong
Ringo was the one who held on.

Hope is not just a word
You can be as free as a bird
Fly to heaven but your memories stay
Down on Earth where you used to play.

Many lives have changed
Since those songs were played
You and I know the truth
Happiness. There is my proof.

They caused the brightest of smiles
Their amount of songs could go on for miles

Whilst the light advances
Others don't even give any chances.

The great ones never die
Their memories will always fly
Way up there above the moon
New legends will come soon.

So let's wait for however long
And hope we weren't wrong
That there will be more
Like these legendary four.

Hope on a new star
And do not look far
For it is not over
Just hold your four-leaf clover.

It's all for one and one for all
They'll never fall
Songs and fans will keep them alive
All they do is thrive.

Naomi Jenkins (10)

Not Just For Kids!

Lovers strolling hand in hand.
Sunshine smiling and beaming on the land.
The see-saw gently rocking to and fro.
The park is not just for kids you know!

The swings cry out with the gentle strain, as they try to reach the planes.
Writers beavering away for hours.
Bees playing hide-and-seek in the flowers.
The park is not just for kids you know!

The great big oak tree slowly groans,
Watching teenagers play on their phones.
Computer geeks flying their bird-like drones.
The park is not just for kids you know!

Mummies chattering as children bravely play.
The birds chirp hello to a beautiful day.
Artists capture the idyllic scene.
The park is not just for kids you know!

The roundabout, feeling a little queasy.
Hay fever sufferers feeling sneezy.
Ladybugs taking it easy, they can be a little lazy.
The park is not just for kids you know!

Pensioners sit and take a pew, as they enjoy the view.
Butterflies flutter in the sky so blue.

Toddlers losing a naughty shoe.
The park is not just for kids you know!

So next time you visit your local park,
As you listen to the crazy dogs bark,
Take a moment, breathe in the scene.
The park is not just for kids you know!

Hannah Fullerton (10)

Spring Poem

Petals and leaves opening up, showing the signs of lovely spring

I see a vision of a bird fluttering past the gentle green trees

I gasp at what's surrounding me, the world is turning better than it has been

To me, the world is waking up

I say to winter "Goodbye, including hot chocolate in a cup!"

Jolly good springtime!

Little bunnies hopping all around
Making quite a squeaky sound
Nibbling on lettuce,
Carrots too
They're so cute
Bouncing in the sky
So blue
I wish I had a rabbit too, do you?

Oh, *plip, plip, drip* and *drop*

Go raindrops from the sky
Showering the earth with life blooming bright
Wet umbrellas splashing by

Plip, plop...

Jolly good springtime!

Dragonflies at the corner of the land
Past my shoulder, past my hands

Lambs are born and
Spring is nearer than before

Earth gets decorated more and more.

Amelie Ngo (6)

Holiday In London

I went to London for a holiday
There were so many sights to see every day.

At every hour of time
That's when Big Ben would chime.
We saw Buckingham P and thought how wonderful it would be
To stand there on the balcony.

We watched the horse parade
As we stood in the shade
And saw the guards walk to and fro
Smartly dressed from head to toe.

We saw St Paul's Cathedral, it was so majestic and great,
We went past on a red London bus that was numbered eight.

On the London Eye, we did spy from up high.
Looking down at the Thames as the ships sailed by.

At Trafalgar Square, the pigeons stare
At the food I have for lunch.
I look inside their deep, dark eyes and let them have a munch.

The Trafalgar Square lions with their heads pointed up
Look like they are frozen in stone... let's just hope they don't wake up.

The towering buildings of London are bigger than the London Eye
But the Shard is the tallest of all with its tip piercing the sky.

As all good things come to an end,
Wave goodbye to Euston Station as our train turns a bend.

Isabelle Morton

An Opportunity Of Life

You may say "Knock-knock" but nobody is there
You've tried again and again
But you can't find them anywhere

What are you looking for...
Or what are you seeking to find...?
As hard as you try the result is nothing
While others are awarded and rejoicing

But what do you do...?
Not just sit there, but you,
Get back up
You wipe away tears
Break a leg
But you have to carry on
Because you know that nothing is done

You may say "Knock-knock" but nobody is there
But what do you do...?
You knock elsewhere because
No one's gonna help
When you fall on the ground
Or get an attack
Even have a setback
Who will cry for you
Help you
Babysit or think about you...?

You can sit on your couch and eat your muffin
Or get back up and do something,
Anything,
Because you're slumping
Is becoming
Something distressing...
I won't be jumping
Because your procrastinating
Will cost you an opportunity in life...

For you may say, "Knock-knock"
When nobody's there
And what should you now do?
Knock... else... where...

Freedom Mayemba

British Wildlife

The amazing animals, that roam the Earth,
All of us are excited with a newborn birth!
We are filled with glee and joy,
Wait... it is a baby boy!

The phenomenal plants and flowers that give us air,
You could grow your own if you dare!
Then you watch the seedling grow and grow and grow,
Wow, a lovely sight you want more so again you sow!

The beautiful birds that watch upon us, way up high,
In a flock, they all stupendously in sync, fly!
But some are in great danger of being forever gone,
So, we have got to protect them to let them live on.

Now, come the fantastic fish that jump and flow,
In the oceans some are high up, some down low.
Most of our world is filled with water and dancing fish.
Some illegally hunted and eaten greedily on a dish.

Now stand up to save the awesome creatures,
With so many we do not appreciate their first-class features.
From the smallest of ants to the biggest of whales
If we all do our bit, then we will succeed not fail.

Lastly, as you choose,
Let them live

Or you will lose
So, if the latter, all will be a myth...

Jack Hei Lee (11)

Farewell, Thomas Buxton

Farewell and bye, old school
Time to move from Thomas Buxton into the next phase of our lives
The time is right
Eight years have flown by with great memories and sweet berries
Primary school is over, we are running over
We had plans but in March 2020 we left school in unprecedented times
What should have been a celebration came to a halt
A time of fear, worry and isolation

Nursery and reception, crawling, moulding, holding and comprehending
Years 1 and 2, forming, shaping, struggling and falling
Years 3 and 4, conforming, strolling and nothing but learning
Years 5 and 6, running, excelling, achieving and striving

Goodbye, playground
Goodbye, classroom
Goodbye, hallway
And whoop whoop, Friday!

We are moving on, it's time to go
Thank you, Sir
Thank you, Miss
And thank you all

So it's with cherished memories
We all go out the door
With great hope and expectations
For what our lifetime holds in store.

Umar Hussain (11)

The Virus

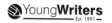

There once was a wizard, who made a potion,
Little did he know he set wheels in motion,
He created a bug, he called COVID-19,
It was teeny tiny, it couldn't be seen,
It went up his nose and made him sick,
He went to the hospital to get help quick.

But COVID did not want to go,
It went to his lungs, and started to grow,
A cough, a sneeze,
A grumble, a wheeze,
The wizard grew sicker,
COVID grew quicker.

Within days the wizard had gone,
Little did we know he had set off a bomb!
COVID spread fast and quick,
Making many, many people, very, very sick.

We were asked to stay inside to keep us well,
How long will this last? No one can tell,
Weeks went by,
Then one day a rainbow appeared in the sky,
The heroes came down all wearing blue,
It is our doctors and nurses to help us through.

Working day and night to defeat all odds,
These heroes are the true gods.

Here is where the story ends,
We can now see our family and our friends.

Thank you, key workers and NHS,
You have saved us all, now get some well-deserved rest.

Amelia Craven

Idolise

A person who inspires me,
A question not to be answered trivially,
It's easy to get caught in the moment,
And answer with someone I don't even know well,
And though they might have played a part,
They didn't fully shape us into who we are,
On the contrary,
Ironically,
It's easy to forget to say,
The people who inspire every day,
Those who work,
Try,
Sun or dirt,
And sometimes only just get by,
That all said once again,
These people didn't mould us into who we became in the end,
And sure their input might have helped in a way,
Yet giving credit where it's due is something we should learn to say,
Even if it might seem self-obsessed,
The answer is what I've experienced best,
In short - the person I idolise,
Is someone I'll know throughout my entire life,
A person who's learnt when to change,
To thrive,

With a range
Of feelings to live to the fullest whilst alive,
In happy times,
Through sad rhymes,
In even sickness or health,
The person I idolise is my future self.

Lucy Higgins

My Family's Dog

My family's dog,
With soft fur of black and white,
When she's really hyper,
You must keep her in sight.

She barks and plays all day,
She always wants attention,
She'll get her own way,
It's only her that you can mention.

My family's dog,
With soft fur of black and white,
When she's really hyper,
You must keep her in sight.

When she's eating food,
You shouldn't come near,
She'll rage into a mood,
It's not growling you want to hear.

My family's dog,
With soft fur of black and white,
When she's really hyper,
You must keep her in sight.

We all love her loads,
She's such a funny dog,
Especially when she's chasing toads,
That makes us laugh as loud as a hog.

My family's dog,
With soft fur of black and white,
When she's really hyper,
You must keep her in sight!

Lina Sounni (8)

We Will Always Remember

The silence that comes as we remember,
Two whole minutes on the 11th of November.

Tears were shed and lives were lost,
Yet all over with the winter frost.

The symbol of the end of the war,
A scarlet poppy of course.

They're sold in Britain today,
For all the men who marched away.

Their petals so soft and red,
For the blood our soldiers shed.

And the seeds in the centre so black,
For the men who didn't come back.

If we forget, lives were lost in vain,
Thanks to them war won't happen again.

Men have died and women were widowed,
So, it's our duty to say...

We will always remember!

If you listen during the silence,
You can just about hear the whispers.

Like old and thankful voices,
Singing from the land above.

Thank them. Pray for them, and remember...

If we forget, lives were lost in vain,
Thanks to them war won't happen again.

Men have died and women were widowed,
So, it's our duty to say...

We will always remember!

Olivia Bowley (11)

Lockdown

We're all at home
As it's the best place to be
Under government lockdown
Isolation, family, friends, you and me
Homeschooling without our
Teachers and friends
This pandemic sooner or later
Has to end
The whole world has changed
In a matter of weeks
For a cure, researchers
are yet to seek
The NHS ploughing through
For the sick and all
Doctors, nurses, keyworkers
Thursday shout outs to you, we call
Weekly shopping is a chore
Two metres apart until you
Get to the door
Nothing on the shelves to buy
Rice, pasta, toilet roll, oh my!
Wearing masks and gloves
Wherever we go
The old, the sick, the vulnerable
With their immunity so low

At the end of this tunnel there is light
A little hope, prayers and we will fight
That one day this will all go away
And we can go back to normality
Running in the playground, hooray!

Janan Sabir (10)

Seasons

Once a year,
Spring comes near,
It's when the nights are grey,
And the sun's at bay,
It's when the flowers have grown,
And the grass is covered in dew,
All the fear is washed away,
On a lovely, sunny spring day.

Once a year,
Summer comes close,
Lots of people like it the most,
It's when the sand is dry,
And you can get fried,
It's when there are topless men,
And ladies looking at them,
Drink lots of water and you'll be fine,
In the glorious summertime.

Once a year,
Autumn's near,
It's when there are bright red leaves,
Falling off the trees,
It's when all you hear is rain,
Which drives you quite insane,

Make sure you stay nice and warm,
In an autumnal rainstorm.

Once a year,
Winter comes close,
Make sure to put on a coat,
It's when children get excited,
And families are united,
It's when presents are bought,
And turkeys are caught,
So put up your tree,
And we'll all agree,
That winter is as cold as can be.

Maya Boden (12)

Tribute To The NHS

NHS, thank you for all the time and effort and lack of rest,
For all of you work from north, east, south and west.
That's why you are rated as the very best.
Us British people are very blessed
For all the COVID-19 tests.

When people want to catch a bus,
You are the one who cuts down the fuss.

People are now in a rush,
About how to find an anti-virus
For the Coronavirus.

When people are trying to get more food,
Once they have chewed,
And you are in a good mood,
You do your job even if people are being rude.
The ambulances go and pursue.
Ventilators cannot be unscrewed.

You are the country's heroes
As you are saving lives,
And many people are still being wives.
As patients are the one who struggle to survive
You are the ones who help them revive.

So, as a country, we just want to say thank you to you.

Saif Nadeem (14)

The Ocean

The ocean and its creatures
So vast that it is boundless
No one will hear your scream
Except those who will immerse you in your dream
For the creatures of the big blue
Are massive compared to you
And they show bloodlust too
Others remain at bay
While in the depths you drown and sway
Nothing could stop the bloodlust
Even one who has lost so much
You start to lose your breath
You will never return hearth
Your mouth opens unwillingly in an attempt to breathe
All the while your legs are trapped so you heave
Then the black void of painlessness approaches
You greet it, rather than reproach from it
And once you pass, there's no return
Was it wise to give up on life and yearn?
For you gave up a brilliant invention
That of which are we blessed only once in turn
Congratulations, in smouldering smoke
Your intentions were corrupt and broke
You've brokered a deal with the devil
And now, you face immortal peril.

Freddie Parker (14)

March 2020

It was March 2020
Nature's own month
After so many months of winter
The sun shone
Birds sang with bees buzzing around
The sky was clear and blue
Morning's arrived early
There was a chill in the air
Winter was gone but the memory's still here
The scent of flowers filled the air
Everybody waiting impatiently for spring
But oh! What did it bring?
Not a soul insight
The streets were empty
People have been put on lockdown
To protect close and dear ones
Young people had to study online
As schools were closed down
No more meetings or family gatherings
As social distancing was the new norm
Although gardens were filled with flowers aplenty
The parks were empty
Only a rare few ventured out during this plight
Despite all the scenes of despair and chaos
Critters chattered playfully

While new shoots found their way through the ground
Trees were filled with leaves
Leaves were green and flowers blooming
It was March 2020...

Sonakshi Devi Seetohul

The Grief, The Pain, The Change

Luscious green trees turn,
As my view of soft grass above
Turns into a horrible mixture
Of mud and blood;
A war-torn earth, a world of gunshot soil,
That is what I see now.

The birds singing from the trees
Is silenced by the ear-splitting shriek
Of gunfire from above
And the sound of cracking twigs and branches,
As the young soldiers march off
To their ultimate doom.
Weather-beaten boots squelching in the mud.
That is what I hear now.

Rough soles on feet perpetually stomping
Right on top of me,
Murdering the few surviving creatures.
Jagged claws, once beautiful nails,
Falling left, right and centre,
As bayonets and guns are dropped.
A kingdom of corpses lies on my surface.
That is what I feel now.

A river of fear and grief
Flows through every solider,
As they march reluctantly on,
Hands and feet trembling.
A dying world, a land of broken timber,
An unrecognisable forest, a barren wasteland.
That's what I am now.

Liam Brady (11)

Earth To Unintelligence

Earth to Unintelligence
Our Earth is in danger.
To it, we are all strangers.
Aliens started contacting us a few years ago by sending a message to Earth.
NASA picked it up but didn't heed to it so now see where it will lead to.
Global warming, climate change, was it not enough?
The Earth is screaming out to us.
Why do you ignore it?
We're putting our fate into the jaws of unpredictable robots,
And nature has decided to betray us as we did with them.
Make change. But we won't.
Step outside your comfort zone and see what we were before, like the peaceful Amazonian tribes.
Mother Nature is giving us one last chance.
But we blew it.
Now I predict our future. Floods and tsunamis.
Animals' Ark. Unforgiving tragedy.
Bask in your treacherous glory and think what was I before?
What have I become?
No turning back now. No Planet B.
Now put your hands together for your greatest destroyer.
COVID-19!

Reeyarani Kaur (14)

The Midwinter Night's Dream

It is a cold, chilly, dark monstrous, sinister night,
There is something about it that gives you quite a fright.
It is a long way until there is the break of light.
Through the stormy winds, I drag my feet with all my might!

I come upon a house, maybe there will be a ghost,
If I go in, I'll inevitably become toast!
Or, blood-loving vampires, I really hate them the most.
With them, I'll be sure to become a lovely tea, roast!

I know that the house will be packed full of sin,
Nevertheless, I will be brave and go in.
The door shut itself like a magnetic pin.
Ahhhhh, promptly, I see a man, with gruesome skin!

This cannot be happening, this must be a dream,
It's impenetrable night here, thicker than steam.
And, I need food, although I hate it, I'll eat cream.
Please, I just need a little spark or speck of gleam!

Jack Hei Lee (11)

Change

I'm tired.

Tired of lies
Tired of the complaints
Revolving around immigrants
I'm tired of having to live in fear
I'm tired of knife crime
I'm tired of the constant blaming
I'm tired of Brexit
There needs to be a change
I'm tired of the one perspective views
I'm tired of fake news
I'm tired of the judging
I'm tired of the strong dislike
That is passed down generation to generation
There needs to be a change
I'm tired of seeing tears on the face of a child
I'm tired of the stereotypes
I'm tired of seeing unhappy smiles
I'm tired of poverty
There needs to be a change
I'm tired of seeing people begging
I'm tired of the government not being MAD enough (making a difference)
I'm tired of the lack of communication
I'm tired of the battles that other countries are facing

There needs to be a change
There
Needs
To
Be
A
Change.

Afusat Olamide Akinsemoyin (15)

The Frontline Nurse

I know you're scared but we are too
We are dependent, we are relying on you
You may find it hard to be content
And have no time or space to vent

The days may be long,
The nights feel like they have no end
No corner to hide in
To every patient you attend

You may wish to cry and that is fine
We need to understand that our health may decline
Returning to our homes we must stay
To protect the world, we must keep away

During the challenging times ahead
With the Coronavirus pandemic spread
And to you, it may not look this way
But you are saving lives each and every day

We are proud of you for your commitment
Your bravery, courage and dedication
With a deep breath, you walk in to care
You are an inspiration

Always remember the sun will rise
Even though you may feel you need to hide

There will be a shine and in the shadow you will emerge
A reflection of the frontline nurse.

Talhah Khan (11)

My Home

Home is a place of love
Home is a celebration
Home is just amazing
Home is a feeling
Home is warm and full of warmth
Home is where dreams come true
Home is joyful
Home is where the cat is
Home is where the dog is
Home is full of respect
Home is like a library
Home is mysterious
Home is a poem full of rooms
Home is with my family
Home is arty
Home is my friends
Home is my brother being annoying
Home is school
Home is where Mum is
Home is enjoyable
Home is a living space
Home is a nap place
Home is laughter
Home is homework
Home is my world

Home is a time machine
Home is where the heart is
Home is watching basketball
Home is where the story begins
Home is full of pets
Home is a teacher
Home is a happy place
Home is a building
Home is a place cared for
Home is a familiar destination
Home is loud sometimes quite
Home is full
Home is scented candles
Home sweet home!

Chloe Emma Lyons (13)

Is This Normal?

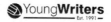

What does it mean to seek the light of joy,
Through the raw emotions which slowly destroy?

Is this normal?

Why, in the depths of swallowing sorrow,
Does pleasure seep through like the dusk of tomorrow?

Is this normal?

How do those thorns of happiness not prick,
Hanging off the wilted rose of grief so wretchedly sick?

Is this normal?

Where does one lose oneself in those wet smiles,
Or in cries where water is begged for by pained eyes?

Is this normal?

When does one learn to stop drinking the pain?
Its taste sour, sweet the delight hard to contain.

Is this normal?

Who understands the glee of standing still?
But the suffocation when one won't move on: a slow kill.

Is this normal?

Should one expect the harrowing insecurity
And the burning desire for an answer of real purity?
The question. The question. The question:

Is this normal?

Adeena Khan

My Best Friend

We were once strangers,
I never thought we would end up as best friends.

Either way, I hope our friendship never ends,
Because you are, and you always will be, my best friend.

When someone hurts you,
I will be here to defend you.

When you have so many worries,
I will be here to listen.

When you are angry,
I will be here for you to let off steam.

When you are confused,
I will be here to help figure things out.

When you need to get away,
I will be here, so we can go together.

When you are in tears,
I will be here to wipe them away.

When you need someone to be there,
I will be here greeting you with a smile.

When you need a change,
I will be here to change with you.

When everyone leaves you,
I will still be here.

I will stay with you,
Even when we're ghosts.

Because you were there for me,
When I needed you the most.

Olivia Misty Johnson (13)

If...

If you can dream and meet goals, you can accomplish more.

If you can stay calm when things get out of hand and go wrong, you can be at peace.

If you can keep going when there's nothing left inside, just remember 'you are worth it!'

If you can hold tight when life's roller coaster goes downhill, then you are really brave.

If you can listen to your friends and to yourself, you will be more considerate of others.

If you can have faith and don't hate yourself, then you can be the better person.

If you can be honest when all around you is a jumble of lies, then you can have belief in yourself.

If you can think before you speak, then you will be thoughtful of others.

If you can stand up tall when those around you fall, then you will be a giant.

And what's more, you'll be a woman, my daughter!

Jessica Niven (12)

Being A Teen

Are you keen
On being a teen?
As much as it's a privilege,
It comes with an image!

An image with stereotypes,
An image with the fake types.
An image with identity,
And social media, especially.

Partying and having fun,
Is always something that must be done.
Shopping and relationships,
Are always such a tough one.

As much as there are positives,
There are also many negatives.
With peer pressure and mental health,
Or bullying and physical health.

Which bag should I use?
Which dress should I choose?
Is it too tight?
Is it too bright?
Or is it as expensive as everybody else's?

Being a teen is super,
As it's the path leading straight into our future!

Taylor Woolcott (13)

Iron Man

Tony Stark was a genius inventor
He knew lots of things
What he knew mostly was that he was
IRON MAN

He made a suit in the enemy army prison
The silver suit was old and rusty
He made the suit to stay alive
He made the suit to save his life
He made the suit to escape the prison

He broke free from the cave prison
He fought the enemy
And he won the battle
He blasted home for freedom

He went to rescue people
He wanted to be loved
But the people, they were frightened
Because his silver suit was scary

He sprayed his suit
It was red and golden
It was sleek and stylish
It was cool
It was shiny
It was awesome

His suit was perfect
He is the invincible Iron Man.

Elvis Terakopian Watts (7)

Smiling At Nature

Sometimes nature's pull is too strong.
I feel a constant need to be connected.
My soul is old, it's been far from nature
For way too long.

The birds witter in an ancient tongue
That I somehow recall knowing.
I could sit and listen to their song for hours
And yet I won't understand what has been sung.

The trees are the oldest family, spanning generations.
Even in their stagnant state, they speak of unknown wisdom.
Their leaves whisper age-old secrets, but they're too quiet to hear.
They have seen the changing between eras, the battles of nations.

But I'm just sitting here, taking all of it in,
The smell of earth and the freshness in the air,
Smiling at nature as my innate love grows within.

Faith McNamara

Is It A Dream?

Is it a dream?
Am I in a dream?
It is probably a dream!
I believe it is a dream! I believe it!

I want to arise every morning with my heart beating,
I want to anoint my heart with stimulation of your strength,
I want to see the god in you rise up filled with veins of a superhuman.
I want to be caught up in rapture by your side with my spear protecting your throne.
I want to wipe my fears and doubt and be awakened by the Black Panther.
Infused with your spirit of love, strength and sense of stride.

Forever you are the glinting diamond, you are the ripened sun, the soft shining star.
I am awake, I am awake, no longer in the dream, no longer in doubt
I can feel your fast running skills, I can feel the strength in your voice
I believe my hero lives forever
Wakanda, rest in power.

Peace Ejodamen (10)

The Scarecrow

The scarecrow's job is a tough one, you know
What they say, the scarecrow's job is never done
He has plenty of things to say
But stuffed with straw and hay, never a word said he
A scarecrow's job is to scare away crows
For they eat crops, those little winged foes
He has plenty of things to say
But stuffed with straw and stuffed with hay, never a word said he
He could see the children playing all day
He wanted to talk to the children but not a word he could say
He has plenty of things to say
But stuffed with straw and stuffed with hay, never a word said he
Fifty years from now, you never know a scarecrow's mouth could never close
For he would talk and talk from day to night, that would definitely be a sight.

Roxanne Magra (10)

While In Lockdown

My eyes fixed on a mysterious image
Like a painting with no meaning, no backstory
And an unidentified artist.
The blue sky and greenery are as a blank white canvas.
No wind to stroke that grass and branches
And dance with decaying leaves across the sky.
The clouds seem to have forgotten how to travel,
Their endless journey has to be put on pause.
As lifeless as a corpse and dense instead of light and bright,
They seem to be sinking instead of floating.
Not a soul to bring character to a story on a normal day,
Or to make the green seem more vibrant.
Not even the birds remembered to wake the flowers as they harmonise.
Not even the clocks could tell the time of day.
The weather fits into no season.
The sun couldn't brighten up this dull image.
In lockdown.

Abigail Greaves

Once Upon A Dream, I Dreamt For A....

Once upon a dream, I dreamt for a unicorn,
My dad said to make a dream come true, you must put your mind to it,
And then I learned,
Not to just wait, and keep my music on.

I knew God loved me so I decided I do some good deeds,
I played with my dog,
Gave money to people in need,
And prayed to God, I wish I had a unicorn.

I kept working hard,
Got a bank card,
Broke a rod,
And prayed to God, I wish I had a unicorn.

As I grew older,
And very much bolder,
On a beach in Scotland,
I see unicorn herds forming circles around me.

It was a dream come true,
It was worth what seemed like two centuries,
Which had many memorable memories.

To make a dream come true, you must put your mind to it,
To make a dream come true,
You must not quit.

You can make your dream come true...

Aisha Maraicar (11)

Bobby The Black Labrador

I feel the sandpapery lick of his tongue on my hand,
He swims in the water but likes it better on land.
His wet paws pad along when we walk,
"Food, food, food," he would say if he could talk!
He is very fast, he's off in a dash,
And then when he's all tired out he comes back in a flash.
He goes to sleep very late at night,
And wakes up early and it's not even light!
The beach is his favourite place to be,
Especially when he's swimming in the sea.
His favourite toy is his bone,
He likes to chew on it when he's alone.
When his tail wags he is the happiest of all,
He would look cute in a scarf or a shawl.
Have you guessed which animal he is?
He's a dog of course!

Elizabeth Lee (11)

I Wish

I wish I had a puppy
Who is soft, cute and fluffy
He will be a mighty husky

When I try to study
He would be my naughty buddy
I hope he doesn't get very muddy

He would climb up on the roof
Look down at me and say his big woof
And act like a real goof

One fine day
I will take him to the park to play
Hours and hours there we will stay

I first thought he would smell yucky
But I will be the one who is very lucky
Who knows, he might like the fried chicken from Kentucky

When I don't play and ignore
He will roll on the floor
Rolls and rolls till he reaches the front door

I wish I had a puppy
Because all of this will make me happy!

Carmel Gabriella Dominic (9)

COVID-19

The time when the world came to a
standstill.
Coronavirus, known as COVID-19.
Year 2020...
No more shaking hands
Don't touch your face.
Never stand too close in a crowded place.
A virus is among us,
Crowding our land.
Jumping from one to another,
Just by the touch of our hands.
We are now at war with an enemy unseen.
We can all stay safe
If we keep our hands clean.
Doctors and nurses doing their duties,
Some feel sick, some must carry on fighting the battle.
We must all keep safe.
Homeschooling wasn't easy,
I missed my friends and my school teachers.
I'm feeling happy and afraid at the same time
Going back to school with this virus still in the air.

Kiran Kaur (10)

When Will I Be Heard?

When will I be heard?
When will I be heard?
My life's been sad and now it's proud.
I've travelled long journeys on the emotional roller coaster.
I've brought my feelings with me, guilt, joy, anger.
Guilt for jealous and anger for not being heard and proudness for who I am.
When will I be heard?
When will I be heard?
The Judge has said adoption so adoption it may be.
The anger I felt has flown away, and now I see a bridge up before me.
When will I be heard?
When will I be heard?
I see the light upon the stars.
The journey may seem scary but exciting it may be.
When will I be heard?
When will I be heard?
The bridge has pulled me forwards and now I can see my arisen waiting up before me.
When will I be heard?
When will I be heard?

Demi Sansom-Jones (10)

Lockdown 2020

Stay safe! Stay safe and wash your hands,
We are all at home, like everyone else across the land.

The NHS is fighting this virus,
We support them, clapping in chorus.

Shopping slots are few,
Remember to use less toilet paper when you go to the loo.

Mum is great,
But a school teacher? Well, that is another debate!

I miss my family and friends,
But I will see them when all this ends!

Chocolate has become a treat,
And Mum takes us cycling along the streets.

Zoom is great for catching up with friends,
Until the free 45 minutes ends.

Hand sanitiser and bleach are Mum's best friend,
Until this crisis comes to an end!

Jessica Louise Hendricks (10)

The Flu-Like Virus

All around wet markets were,
rats and bats and animals with fur,

The Chinese ate without a clue,
that their new snacks would cause a flu,

A flu that was contained at first,
a flu that soon became the worst.

By eating a bat, a virus created,
lockdown was mentioned and couldn't be debated,

A week at home became a bore,
all the people inside didn't like it any more,

Two hours to the beach in the car,
Boris had warned not to travel so far.

People got sick; people got ill,
eventually, the government couldn't afford the bill,

The NHS worked as hard as they could,
but the people were dying quicker than they should,

Ventilators were short, hospital beds too,
thousands of people dead all because of a flu.

Grace Broadbent

My Little Pony Iris

My little pony Iris was as white as snow,
The saddest day of my life was when she had to go,
The vet said she'd lost her teeth, she could not eat her hay,
She was also very old and lame, and she had had her days,
She called us with a greeting when she saw us come,
A few hours later, a man came with a gun,
Trustingly, she stood there as he gently scratched her head,
I turned my back, heard a bang and Iris lay there dead,
For days and days I cried, had what I done been right?
But I just couldn't let her suffer through another winter's night,
Up in Heaven's pastures I hope she's young, strong and free,
For a ponies paradise, there surely must be.

Lexxi Nelson

My Sister, Zuna

She is cool, she is gentle, she is kind
Sometimes she's arrogant but never mind
I couldn't agree more to she's the best sister ever
Me and her, her and me, we're the best team together
Why shouldn't I look up to her?
She's better than any sort of frankincense or myrrh
The sad thing is I don't see her much anymore
And without her honestly, I am feeling quite poor
I have no one to tell me what I should wear to school
I don't want to lose her, she is like a precious jewel
Though I know she hasn't forgotten me
I know she wouldn't, why would she?
But it doesn't mean I don't miss her company
I always will, she is the greatest sister
And everyone should know her name is Zuna.

Misha

Making Magic

A fairy reached up in the sky
On her tiptoes so high
There, a lovely star she found
To put upon her fairy wand.

With a twinkle in her eyes
The little fairy always tries
To make some magic sweet and clear
For all she, in her heart, holds dear.

Just make a wish, you never know
You may be blessed but by the fairy and her wishing star
Be she here or be she far
For wishes have their own bright wings
The soul, its beautiful music sings
Light touches light so far and you
Together, make your own dreams come true.

Wishes, make wishes it will come true
Make sure you believe in magic
And fairies then your dreams come true.

Rebekah Gooden

Yay! Spring Has Arrived!

The nation watched spring arrive
While the world watched the Earth survive
As we sat by our windows to take five

Yay! Spring has arrived!

All you can hear is the buzzing of the bees
And the birds in the trees

As the sun shone
The world was in lockdown
Feeling rather rundown

But the scent of the flowers
Grew under the rainbow showers
As we keep watching all of man's powers
With superpowers!

Yay! Spring has arrived!

This is the best spring I've had
When spring is over, I will be sad
But for now let's be glad
Of the time we had
Watching spring arrive
And the world revive.

Jessica Hodsdon (12)

The Magical Land Of Dreams

The magical Land of Dreams
Is the place where all your dreams come true
You could be floating in the magical stream
Or you could turn blue
One day I was eating candyfloss
Just minding my own business
When all of a sudden, I turned into the boss
The boss of Dreamland, oh my goodness
Oh I do hate being a boss
I'd rather be doing the floss
Quick, quick wake up, wake up
This is not at all a fun dream
With a quick flash, I turned into a cup
And you'll never guess who was drinking me, only my football team!
What did I hear in the distance? A massive thunderstorm
Let's hope this will make me leave this magical land
I woke up in my bed which is lovely and warm
Oh no, not really, I was sinking in quicksand!

Albie Batchelor (9)

Stop The Blood

Let's all help this innocent Earth,
This is what God said - the One and Only who created our birth.
People every day are dying from bombs and guns,
Girls and boys, dads and mums.
This happens in Syria, Iraq, Yemen and even more,
They face the pain and bare the gore.
We have luxurious houses and well-built walls,
We have top restaurants and big rich malls.
The poor must eat old dirty mud,
They have infected scars dripping with blood!
They do not have proper help or medical aid,
But we own cars, cleaners and maids.
We have armed policemen and doors which lock,
The poor do not have defence and they are at risk of getting shot.
I hope this poem has changed your mind!
To give donations and to be more kind.

Waasil Sidik (11)

Quarantine Poem

Essential items only,
Oh, how we feel so lonely.
Nowhere to go,
No one to see,
But this is how it has to be.

Exercising all the time,
Some at home drinking wine.
Waiting for the pubs to open,
And sports to start back up,
Luckily it's not the year of the FA Cup.

Going out but social distancing,
Realising important things.
No GCSEs,
Worrying about our futures,
Occasional calls from our tutors.

Missing friends,
I hope this ends!
It shouldn't be this way!
It's going to be very strange,
But we all root for big change.

Although the grass is really green,
I hate quarantine!

Annalise Foley (16)

All About Me

Sparkly and pink always catches my eye
Bags, shoes, clips and bows I mostly buy
Hop, skip and jump, aiming at the biggest puddles
How I wish the water splashing out would turn into bubbles
I could pop the muddy bubble and ask everyone
It's chocolate spread on my sweet face, like a taste anyone?

Butterflies and flowers I've mastered to draw
Mommy says my family drawing deserves a high score
I've just turned four, I feel I have grown
I chat with my soft toys in every tone
Bears, dinosaurs, dolphin, big and soft, I like to snuggle
Parents and my two brothers are always ready for a cuddle
I'm the princess here at home everyone highly adores
Love you, Mom and Dad, little princess forever yours.

Safiyyah Shafraz-Abubakar (4)

The Animal Journey

Snake, Snake, slithering snake,
Eating all my birthday cake,
What a horrible mess you make!

Croc, Croc, stuck under a rock,
Munching mud from off a block,
Giving people an enormous shock!

Shark, Shark, lost in the park,
Getting scared of the dusky dark,
Crying when it hears a dog bark!

Fox, Fox, chillin' in his box,
Painting patterns on his socks,
Stealing food from the docks!

Cow, Cow, saying, "Meow!"
Thinking that it's a cat right now,
But that would be a wow!

Goat, Goat, in a moat,
Setting sail in his milky boat,
In order to stay afloat!

Hattie Boxall (9)

The Door

Dark oak door held together with flowering vines,
The key troubling to get,
You had to resist your heartbroken whines,
Deal with the devil and place a bet,
Scale a mountain of rock,
Fight the gleaming knight of blue,
All for that door you wished to unlock,
Behind that door a wish came true,
A treasure more precious than diamond,
The most colour with indescribable hue,
All to unlock that door,
To find happiness and fulfilment,
True understanding, purpose,
And on that throne of knowledge you can see,
The great traveller, who overcomes,
Sadness, grief
Truly understanding all that they can be.

Liv Strong

Hellos Turned Into Goodbyes

When your love came I couldn't even tell
It could never be the same but went well
Even when it rained my love would never change
Not gonna leave again but you were acting strange

None can compare, trust me, my love is fair
To a beauty so rare, even in thin air
You smell like the most beautiful flower
In the morning you give me more power

But I thought you would fill my life with bliss
But instead you poisoned my heart with stress
Now I am heartbroken and depressed
Even though it hurts, I'm still over obsessed

But as it's all over now
It's time to say goodbye.

Angelika Stepniak

She Was...

She was woven from starlight,
And a flurry of snow,
And a thousand nebulae drifting
Through an endless black hole.
She was borne of moondust,
And a spark of hope,
And the breath of Venus
Intertwined in her soul.
She was painted from violets,
And stained-glass windows,
And the embrace of the winter air
That filled her lungs.
She was made of lace and twilight,
And the moon and fairy lights,
And the sunset reflected
In the iris of her eyes.
She was fashioned of love,
And crisp autumn leaves,
And the way that the sun
Illuminates the dust in the air.
She was begotten of stolen kisses,
In a secluded meadow,
Where our love blossomed
Like the blush of a cherry tree.

Ffion Corbett (15)

Stuck At Home

Now the authorities have declared that the school gates are to shut,
We will need to remain inside our abode even if it's in a hut.

Children like me are now feeling very sad,
We can't go out to play because the pandemic is so bad.

The weather is nice and out comes the sun,
It's unusual that PE now has to be done without a class run.

We need to stay home to protect our community,
Thanks to technology we can contact our friends and keep our unity.

Every day we are making history,
COVID-19 is affecting every country.

Children are learning new skills by studying on Google classroom,
Our daily commute is now from the lounge back to the bedroom.

Mahveen Ana Chowdhury

Race Is Sacred

I don't choose to be black, brown or white
Life is a gift of God and living is my right
If I am black why should I be depressed?
If I am brown why should I be stressed?
Listen to me, oh people, skin on our bodies
Is just like a dress.

Nights are dark and days are bright
They love each other and do not fight
Stop fighting humans and love each other
Forget about the colour and hug like a mother.

This is Savannah, who want to tell to all.
I'm a little girl who doesn't like to fight.
If you like, come with me.
I will show you the light.

I don't choose to be black, brown or white
Life is a gift of God and living is my right.

Savannah Javed (9)

The Eleventh Hour

The battlefield is finally clear
Thank you to those that have sacrificed
Without you the country would have been in fear
And innocent lives would have been sliced

Let us all cheer for the victory
And the brave soldiers that put their hearts to it
This gave us the everlasting liberty
Otherwise our country would have split

Those with courage have passed away
But left us with a peaceful kingdom
Let us ensure the country does not go astray
And make fools become wise in their imprudent wisdom

The country is in our hands now
And the legacy has just begun
Let us join this beautiful fortune and bow
For sorrow has ended and my message is done.

Aisha Suleman (28)

The Annoying Fool

The biggest fool I knew
Sat down next to me on a screw
As I moved my head he did too
And when I looked at his foot he was wearing my shoe
So I turned away and to my surprise
When I turned back he hit me in the eye
So I ran away and ended up on a bridge
But the silly old guy followed me with his fridge
I managed to escape and I felt much better
When I got home I wrote him a letter
So I jumped in bed and my letter read...

'Sparkle, sparkle, wink, wink, wink
Who on earth are you? I think
You are a pumpkin in my sink
And you will always stink, stink, stink.'

Akhil Bhatlapenumarthy

Missing!

Part of me was missing,
I couldn't remember what!
The only thing apparent,
I was missing my left sock!

It was such a dilemma,
I didn't know what to do!
I couldn't just wear one sock,
If I was putting on my shoes!

Did it run away?
Could it have gotten far?
The fact that I am thinking this,
Was a little bit bizarre!

It couldn't have run away!
It couldn't have gotten far!
Perhaps I was a little crazy,
And I was miles off by far!

I am still searching for my missing sock,
But I don't really care!
Now what I am looking for,
Is the gum stuck in my hair!

Katie Duggan (12)

Deal With It

Have you ever wondered
What it's like to sit in a blue, broken chair
To tell a therapist
Have you ever wondered
What's going on
To speak of your awkward situations.

To talk about your family's breaking
To talk about how you get thrown around between parent's houses
To find out your dad's on a dating app
To find out someone's going to be your stepmum
To find out how your dad really behaves indoors
To be told that you're never going to understand
more like, they just don't really want to tell you
You just have to face it
You can't avoid it
So deal with it
Whether you like it or not.

Bani Dhuria (12)

Library

From the heart of the dark,
I could hear the library humming,
The book pages rumbling and authors quietly reading
While thinking of ideas to write.

The owls howling at night,
The birds twittering in the dark night,
The sounds of the cold wind whistling in the dark,
My dad snoring in the back
And the sun being set.

Just got a book from the library for three whole weeks,
I brought it to school and told my teacher to read it with me,
So I crawled up in the chair next to her,
Ready to read it with her,
We both took a big breath and began to read.

Diana Gujdova (13)

Peter Pan

As I make my way
To find my friends
We laugh and play,
It never ends.

Across the night
The stars shine bright,
With Tinker Bell as my guide
She will never leave my side.

Over towns and cities,
Through the trees and leaves,
Over the stormy deep blue seas.

As I arrive back home,
I sense the sorrow has grown,
When children play
Captain Hook makes his way.

We battle and fight
Throughout the day and night,
As I guard and protect
The land of the unknown,
I know in my heart
I'll never be alone.

Auguste Marcinkonyte (14)

COVID-19

Once upon a time,
There was a deadly disease.
It is COVID-19
People are crying
People are dying
The people are panicking
Trolleys are filling
If God is willing
The world is ending
People are defending
And Corona is spreading
Where is your mask?
You've got to think fast
The army is coming
People are running
People are in ICU
And it can just be you
Countries are on lockdown
People are knocked down
Scientists are testing
People are resting
You're always washing
Before what were you thinking
All stop worrying
People are hurrying

People are self-isolating
Prices are spiking
People, are you ready?

Ayaan Rahman (10)

The Rainbow

Go and slide down the rainbow,
Maybe up high there's a cloud,
Or a jet plane,
A leprechaun,
Or a pot of gold.

Go and slide down the rainbow,
Maybe a bird is flying,
Maybe you'll see the sun,
Or an island,
Or the sea.

Go and slide down the rainbow,
If it's raining it will stop.

Go and slide down the rainbow,
Even if there's only time ticking,
Even if there's only a cold breeze,
Even if there's nothing there.
Go and slide down the rainbow.

At least there is a beautiful view.

Oliver Hodgkins (9)

My Handsome Friend

I start by saying that,
My little dog's name is Lucky.
If I call him by his name,
He will always be so happy
And he is the best puppy.

Every day we play together,
And we will have our meals.
We will sleep and sing,
I will care for him as always,
He will care for me.

We are best of friends.
We sometimes miss each other,
As I need to go to school.
But he'll play with my little brother!

My little friend called Lucky.
I care for all your best.
You are my second brother,
I wish you all the best.

George Stefan Gorban (8)

Dear Mum

Oh, Mum, I don't know where to start
Perhaps when you drove me in a shopping cart
Oh, Mum, you taught me to slurp
But after that came a big loud burp
Oh, Mum, your jokes are funny
But I would like to spend your money
Oh, Mum, you keep the house so clean
But I litter everywhere, hidden and unseen
Oh, Mum, when you drive we're always late
But you taught me that this is just fate
Oh, Mum, you should be a cook
But try not to force me to read a book!

Dear Mum,
Thanks for everything,
From your cooking to teaching me to sing.

Abu-Bakr Ismail (9)

Remembrance

Remembrance Day isn't about two minutes' silence.
No. Remembrance Day isn't about boring assemblies.
No. Remembrance Day isn't about giggling and listening to the teacher snap, "Wipe that smile off your face."
No. But. Remembrance Day is about remembering soldiers who fought,
And those whose souls got sought.
Yes. Remembrance Day is about those who fell,
And those who survived living hell.
Yes. Those who fought in the trenches
And longed to be sitting on benches.
Remembrance Day is an important day,
Please do not say hooray.

Micha Max Goldberg (11)

Angel Of Death

He's one of a kind, one that all shall see.
Just wait till the day when all will believe.
He's tall and thin and wears a filthy long cloak,
And you'll finally see as he ties you with his ropes.
Then he pulls your soul, lifting it higher and higher
And he takes you out of this universe and throws you for miles.
It's a disturbing experience, one that all shall see,
So think again next time you don't think before you speak.
Believe it or not, but there is life after death, there is more,
It's a whole new world waiting to be explored.

Hafsah Khan (13)

Never Again

My feet were heavy with a continuous flow of water
Let alone the pulling of the mud beneath my feet.
My friend was hypnotised by the sight
Of the soldiers fighting for their life
On the floor a few feet away from us.
We were fresh out of school
And yet these sights have forever changed our perspective
Of our world at this young age.

How are we meant to forget this?
We gave each other a look of dismay.
But in that short moment
We lost all consciousness of the battle
And one of us lost our life too.
My mouth screamed but the sound was muted,
All my senses lost
And my young friend lost too.

Daisy Alexander (13)

Living In My Skin

Living in my white skin I have a good chance to win,
Living in my black skin I have to work harder to win,
Living in my white skin I'm privileged before I begin,
Living in my black skin I'm waiting for my chance to begin,
Living in my white skin I must be right,
Living in my black skin I'm left to fight,
Living in my white skin I enjoy hanging out with my mates,
Living in my black skin I hang out with my mates, spot-checked, harassed, this world is full of hate,
Living in my white skin opportunities are endless,
Living in my black skin equal opportunities could end this.

Kameron Roulston (13)

One Last River

One last river
3,000 years from now
One last river flows.

The last rising sun
It looks so fun!
For it has seen...
(This is why it beams)
The one last river.

Oh, and those last trees
Rustling their leaves,
Whispering in their secret language
For they have seen the one last river
That flows to the last blue ocean.

The last blue sky
It is so high!
The last fluffy clouds fly
The last clear sky stares down below
To the one last river.

Finally, we come to the last blades of grass
Waving their last glistening dewdrops
For they have seen the
One last river,
The last river...

Eliza Khan (10)

VE Day

R adio - "The ware is over." I'm so happy.
E xcited that the enemy gave up. No more fighting!
S ad because of all those people who died in the war.
P eople will see their families again.
E vacuees - "I will see my mum and dad again!" "We really miss them so much!"
C elebrations! We stayed up late and had fun watching fireworks. They were loud, colourful, red, blue and white. There was lots of food.
T rains. My daddy's coming home on the best steam train I have ever seen.

Brayden Barrett (7)

The Boy Who Fell In The River

On the very brink of a rock-hard cliff,
I saw a wooden skiff,
I couldn't row so I fell in the river,
Then the hunter threw me his quiver,

In the forest I started to shiver,
'Cause I fell in an icy river,
Then I filled the quiver with water,
And threw it back to the hunter,
He launched a gold coin into the river,

Then I caught it with the quiver,
The hunter gave me a big piece of cloth,
When in the river there was a sloth,
I tied on the cloth and jumped out the river,
Then I started to shiver.

Ashwin Narendrakumar (11)

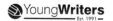

I Am A Guinea Pig

I live in a cage
Until six years of age
I'm always happy to sit on a lap
Sometimes while even having a nap
My favourite time of every day
Is having my owners come my way
I let out an excited squeak
And run to the front in order to seek
Unlike you, I look forward to veggies
Not those disgusting potato wedgies!
I feel sorry for my owner having to pay
For so much hay every single day
But I'm sure they don't mind as I think they are wealthy
And I'm sure they want to keep me happy and healthy.

Marcus Brigden (9)

A Story Of The Night Sky

And when you fall,
You are going to burn the sky;
Your light will be so strong,
That your soul will turn into the brightest,
The brightest light, the brightest star of the sky.

When the moon met the night sky,
She fell in love with his darkness,
So she turned into his light,
And this love gave birth to stars.

The moon was sailing on the sky's endless sea,
Further away than ever,
The waves were lighting up the stars,
While the Earth was tearing up,
At the thought that his love ran away.

Rucsandra Benedek (18)

Spring In Lockdown

The blazing sun shines down
On the wild colourful trees in blossom,
Bikes speed past the carpet of bluebells in the forest
Where trees dance in the wind,
The lambs take their first careful steps on the grass as green as an avocado,
Birds fly gracefully while getting supplies for their nest, chirp, chirp,
Fluffy rabbits leap quickly as high as skyscrapers,
The magnificent fruits grow like there is no tomorrow
Bursting with flavour,
Busy buzzing bees collect the nectar from the rainbow leaf flowers,
Spring is fantastic!

Alfie Brewer (10)

The Strong And Compassionate

Whose dog is that? I think I know.
Its owner is quite angry though.
He was cross like a dark potato.
I watch him pace. I cry hello.
He gives his dog a shake,
And screams I've made a bad mistake.
The only other sound's the break,
Of distant waves and birds awake.
The dog is strong, compassionate and deep,
But he has promises to keep,
Tormented with nightmares he never sleeps.
Revenge is a promise a man should keep.
He rises from his cursed bed,
With thoughts of violence in his head,
A flash of rage and he sees red.
Without a pause, I turned and fled.

Yahye Abukar (14)

COVID-19 Schedule

Joe Wicks in the morning,
stretching, running.
I'm still yawning,
sleepy, tired.

Next: Home School.
We are working,
Skyping cruel tutors,
my eyes rolling.

Fry-up brunch,
chewing, swallowing.
I, and little brother munch,
delicious, enticing.

Zooming mates,
chatting, talking.
Quality of app? Rates!
Now quiet, lonely.

Little brother's hair,
horrific, terrible.
Life isn't fair,
boring, tedious.

BBQ in back garden,
meat, veg,

tummies will laden,
tubby, fat.

NHS we're clapping.
Proud, thankful.
All hands tapping.
Grateful, appreciative

Farrah Mary Cullen

I Call Him My Grandad

I know a special man who's honest and true,
I call him my grandad and he adores everything I do.

My grandad is a soldier and fights a battle every day,
He hates that he can often seizure but his willpower to carry on makes him the greatest achiever.

Whenever he's around, I smile from cheek to cheek,
He always makes me feel so strong because he's never weak.

My grandad is my number one, my hero and my idol.
He has stood by my side as I have grown,
The bravest man I've ever known.

Courtney Sartain (11)

Piano Balloon

Life is a piano balloon,
Which pops when it's out of tune,
Leaves scars for life,
Like a knife.

No single day passes by,
Without the sound of a horse's neigh,
That just proves our theories right,
That not everyone is exactly bright.

Our heart is running a non-stop marathon,
And we find love wherever we run,
Our soul is the main part of our body,
That gives us the weird feeling of sorry.
Life is full of shocking surprises,
But in return, we receive better surprises.

Aina Zahara Humayoon (11)

Mechanical Beasts

They roar along
Not a doubt in mind
Breaking down this earth
Not wasting time
Like a mythical beast
They are out to destroy
Whether it be woman, girl
Man or boy

Who created something
So destructive to the nice?
But now we will pay the price
As what their actions cost
Is our lives

All inhabitants will be lost
It may be too late
It may not
But if we don't change
All will be forgot
Our earth, our species, our creatures
The whole lot.

Toby Leigh

A Man Who's Very Powerful

He started his life
When he was born in 1964
In the city that never sleeps
New York City
You may ask yourself
Why he was born there
The reason being was
His father was studying at Columbia University
But he was an Englishman
How did this famous figure
Start his powerful career as the Prime Minister?
The facts were he was granted both American and UK citizenship
Then in no time at all, in 2019
He became Prime Minister of the UK
And what a roller coaster he's taken.

Abi Harding (13)

Jingle The Bells With Joy

Jingle the bells with joy,
Jingle the bells with hope,
Jingle the bells with kindness
And happiness.

I just want to say,
I want to say,
Jingle the bells with joy,
Jingle the bells with hope,
Jingle the bells with kindness
And happiness.

When you are sad come to the Christmas bells
And they'll cheer you up,
Jingle, jingle, jingle, jingle and
Jingle the bells with joy,
Jingle the bells with hope,
Jingle the bells with kindness
And happiness.

Amy Jane Rockett (9)

Time

Time...
All I need is a little more time...
I find myself in a room with little sunshine
My hands are shaking
Making my pencil start quaking

I begin to pout
I need to get out
I can't do this anymore
I'm losing every bit of form

Then it hits me
The truth about life
An eagle can fly
And humans can try

But sometimes
We can give up
This was not meant to rhyme but
It's easier to write poems when you're running out of time.

Gracie Billings (12)

Journey Through Paradise

The train was chugging along the track,
Now there is no coming back.
India glided past my window,
Trees were blossoming yellow, ripe mangoes.
Cattle surrounded the rickety train,
It was very dry (did it even get rain?).
The sound of mooing,
Was gentle and soothing.
The chirping of birds,
Ringing of bells of the herds.
All the things I could hear,
Were a delight to my ears.
The smell of jasmine filled the air,
I was blinded by the sun's glare.
I felt as refreshed as I can be,
And continued my onward journey with glee.

Nivan Shurpali (8)

Sweet Dreams

Today has been so much fun,
But now it's over, now it's done,
I'll close my eyes nice and tight,
Ready for the big long night.

At 3am there's no cause for alarm,
Nothing to worry, nothing to harm,
The owl glides in his silent flight,
Mouse is well hidden out of his sight.

The early train with passengers few,
Leaves Swindon Station, bound for Crewe,
The birds in the trees are ready to wake,
It's the start of another sunny daybreak.

Georgina Eve Bunnage (7)

Lockdown, Lockdown

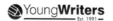

Lockdown, lockdown, I want to go downtown
But now I have a frown, lockdown, lockdown
We all need a crown, lockdown, lockdown

I can't remember a clown
Everything is shut down, lockdown, lockdown
We need a countdown, lockdown, lockdown
We need a rundown, lockdown, lockdown
I have a frown because this feels like a let-down

Lockdown, lockdown, we are all having a meltdown
Lockdown, lockdown, I think we all have a frown
Because of lockdown, lockdown.

David Allan (12)

If I Were A Snail

If I were a snail I would want the whale to take me to Arendelle to meet Elsa and Anna.
I would see a gigantic, super-sized castle with fancy clean windows.
I would smell delicious yummy food.
My favourite food is the sandwiches and the cake.
I would hear beautiful, nice music coming from a band.
I would feel the cold snow so I'd need to wear lovely, cosy gloves, a fluffy coat and some shoes.
I would taste Elsa's special ice cream cone.
It tastes like lemonade.

Ava Lewis (6)

The Clumsy Farting Dragon

There once was a dragon named Rhysy-Poops.
He was as clumsy as a moose.
Forever falling and trumping.
He didn't do very well at jumping.
He would fall over nothing at all
His farts could knock down a wall.
One day he went for a long walk.
He fell over a big lump of chalk.
As he fell down,
His fart made a terrible sound.
But he wasn't embarrassed at all
Even though he knocked down a massive wall.
He saw a clown who was laughing
It seemed to be catching.
He laughed too
And they went to the zoo.

Rhys Oliver Frost (9)

Corona, Corona

Corona, Corona,
Please go away,
Corona, Corona,
You ruined our day.

Corona, Corona,
You are making people poorly,
Corona, Corona,
You are making people sad.
We are mad.

Corona, Corona,
I miss my family,
Corona, Corona,
I miss my friends,
Corona, Corona,
I miss my teachers,
I miss you all.

Corona, Corona,
I miss going out,
Corona, Corona,
Please disappear.
We are in fear.

Aaishah Bint Hussain (7)

Spring In England

After the bare, brown, bony trees,
Comes a season of birds singing in the breeze.
A wonderful blanket of glistening white,
Replaced by meadows of daffodils and sunlight.
Flowers and buds ready to bloom,
The sun is so bright, as bright as the moon.
Oh!
But the weather we're expecting is not to be found;
The grey in the sky is the same as the ground.
Dark, gloomy clouds are filling the sky,
Which should be bright blue, with birds flying by.

Aaryan Thomas-Michael Manarkattu

My Lockdown Poem

Wake up,
Work from home,
Stare longingly out of the window,
What a sunny day...

Wake up,
Work from home,
Why can't we go out and play?

'Stay at home,
Save lives',
That's what they say,
But I think there's going to be a riot some day.

Wake up,
Queue for hours outside
The supermarket,
Wait hours
For public transport,
Coronavirus, one day
You are going to pay.

Wake up,
Go for my daily exercise,
Talk to my friends,
Read in the garden,
Maybe isolation is okay.

Sabrina Kanli (11)

What's On The Top Of The Hill?

On top of the hill
There sat a dog
Then there was a bog
Why were they there?
There was a whistle
There was a sizzle
What to do?
As a shout came
There was a fright
"Aarr!" was shouted with a bite
There was a cow now
And some sheep
A flycatcher
Or you may say a frog
A shout came
Flee
Clatter, batter
What else is there?
A cat, lion and elephant came
Scram, you little thing.

Milly Jones (12)

Roald Dahl

R oyal Air Force pilot to begin with
O il company is where I worked before
A happy home life I lived
L oving Mother told me many stories
D ozens of stories written for adults

D aughters and sons later inspired my work
A book named James And The Giant Peach came along
H ereafter many books to encourage children's imagination
L ong lives my passion to help young people read.

Maliha Rahman (8)

The Brain

Helpless, deep under
Locked away, shut
The pain was dreadful

Crying inconsolably
Couldn't feel anything
Not even the pain I felt

Couldn't hear anything
Not even a beat
I wanted to leave
But I couldn't, I had no feet

Feeling a shiver running
Down my spine
I couldn't stop
I couldn't help
I felt like my life had stopped

And it had for that hour in time.

Amber Nelmes (14)

A Dolphin As A Pet

I'd really like a dolphin as a pet
Although it might be tricky to take it to the vet
I'd love to teach it a trick or two
Like the ones I've seen when I've been to a zoo
Stroking it would be really fun, I bet
But I think I'd get a tiny bit wet
I'd swim with it every day in the sea
Though I think it would be faster than me
But somehow I don't think I'll ever get
A beautiful dolphin as my pet.

Callie Brigden (7)

My 2020

Happy thoughts and laughs out loud,
Being with friends and family.
Things that haven't been found,
Are things that are your fantasy!

Seeing Gran and Grandad,
Travelling to loads of countries.
Reading books about an unknown land,
And lying in on Sundays!

Having fun with my cat,
And watching funny movies.
There's nothing I'll regret,
Especially eating cookies!

I'll be ready for any adventure,
And be proud wherever I enter.

This will be my 2020!

Ava Cassandra Goshei (10)

My Father Is My Hero

My father is my hero.
He is like the sun,
His heart is like a bun.
My father is like a big tree,
Who gives me shelter for free.
My father always helps me,
Wherever and whenever I may need.
He always praises me,
When I do good deeds.
He always gives me a good bath,
And leads me on the right path.
He always keeps me nice and warm,
And no matter what, protects me from every harm.
I am thankful to God that he is my dad,
As now I will try to become just like my dad.

Gurleen Gupta (13)

Autumn

The autumn wind blows the dead leaves away
As the acorns grow day by day.
Autumn is here
And the heavens and skies are no longer clear.
Winter shall follow
Like an oncoming flock of crows.

Harvest is now upon us
As everyone is getting wrapped up in all the fuss.
As crops start to grow
Farmers harvest crops row by row.
Farmers gather carrots, peas, tomatoes,
As well as wheat, beans and potatoes.

As evening arrives
The plant life rots and struggles to survive.

Iqrar Haider

Journey

I practise and practise and practise
My fingers dance across the strings
Leaping over metal knots and hiking over frets
Eventually my fingers reach the end of the fretboard
They just hop onto the next string
And they move string to string until
They reach the sixth string
They just go back and up, down
And reiterate the process
Again and again and again
Then, abruptly they travelled on their quest
To a consummate musical odyssey
Full of upbeat jovial melodies.

Gibran Karim Khan (12)

Marco Polo

M arco Polo was a famous Italian explorer
A long time ago he went to China
R ecorded in the Travels of Marco Polo
C ities and countries he explored
O f all his adventures, I like the China trip

P eking in China is also one of the places he has visited
O ccupation for Marco is exploring
L iving an adventurous life
O f all his adventures, which one do you like?

Ryan Pittoni (9)

The Magnificient Moon

Moon,
Gleaming moon,
I witness your gorgeous face,
High in the sky,
In your place.
Silently you appear,
In the night,
For me to see you when tucked in tight!
You look like a ball of scrumptious cheese,
Floating over a torrential sea,
Waiting to be munched by me,
Oh moon,
It's that time already,
You are going to fade away soon,
And be replaced by the sun,
Here comes day, in which we have plenty of fun,
See you tonight moon,
I wish to see you soon!

Kavin Ravikumar (11)

Once Upon A Dreamy Night

All that turns off is the light
as I get ready for the night.
My pillow has reached pressure by my head,
while my dream carries on being lead.
My dream is lead by an animated path.
I get tucked in tight,
Hoping my dream would give me a laugh.
My dream begins here
as my head starts getting bright.
Within a second my imagination goes flash
into something I am actually in.
Colours everywhere as I wonder around not
knowing where to start.

Amina Ghazi (11)

Forget Me Not

Life is like a flower,
You start off as a seed in a field of the unknown,
And as you grow and your petals bloom
You slowly find yourself,
You're surrounded by many flowers but each is to its own,
Trying your hardest to get through the rainy days and stand up tall,
Some winds are too strong and we don't survive them all,
In the field an empty space lay,
Reminding us where a beautiful flower use to stay.

Jasmin Whitmore (14)

Lockdown

L ockdown matters, stay at home
O ut of sight for a while not keeping in touch, others matter
C aring for families, friends and neighbours
K eeping away from a life-threatening condition
D ifficulties staying at home, not going outside
O nline classes keeping us busy
W ashing our hands and keeping safe
N ow you have to be brave, normal days are what I wait for.

Tashifa Mahmood

How Would You Feel?

Put this into perspective,
Now I am no detective.
But animals are perpetually slaughtered,
Not fed or watered.
This is considerably hindering,
Although there are muffled voices whispering.
But I will not tolerate this contemptuous behaviour,
Animals will not be used for manual labour.
Are you all in favour?
Together we can resolve this deplorable issue,
To conclude, would you like a tissue?

Lola Terry-Corneille

The Tasmanian Tiger

Tigers are ferocious
But they are quite atrocious
If you tease them
But not if you please them
They feast upon carcasses of other animals
But that doesn't mean that they are cannibals
They can be fun
No, they don't chew gum
They live in zoos
So they are provided with food
They sure are Tasmanian
Not quite sure if that's Arabian
Tigers are cool but not if they drool.

Safiyah Iqbal

My Hedgehog

H urrah for my little woodland friend, spiky but ever so sweet,
E very night he comes looking for a treat.
D igging and delving is what he likes best,
G oing back home for a snack and a rest.
E ating slugs, worms and beetles is such a delight,
H owever, for me, I would not like a bite!
O nce you invite this little one home
G lad that you will never roam.

Max Hillgrove

Remembrance Day

Walking across the fields of poppies
Filled with autumn leaves
Consider your ancestors
Being killed in a world war frenzy
Our beloved family risked their lives
To save our country
To this day we think about
The generations before and stand
Two minutes in November
To remember those who fought for us
From this generation onwards, you will lead
Together we can make a world of peace.

Ruwayda Abdulfatah (11)

Life In Lockdown

Life in lockdown is not fun
Coronavirus has left us stunned

There's not much do
So we have to find something new

I hope this virus goes away
Or else we'll end up in dismay

I miss my family and my friends
As the fun never ends

I miss eating out
Without a doubt

As we've had all these turns and bends
I hope this virus comes to an end.

Aashish Toprani (10)

Feelings

It is a touch,
Shaped so accurately,
That is hard to lose.

They are like glue,
They stick to you wherever you go.

They are clouds,
That are unreachable.
They can't be stopped,
Just like time can't.

They are similar to leaves,
Flimsy,
But they can't go away.

They are like hearts,
Use them carefully,
They have broken people.

Aalya Singh Dewan

Not So Cool When You're Not At School

Tick-tock, tick-tock
Time is really going slow today
It's not so cool
When you're not at school today, Miss.

No running in the corridors
No playing in the playground
Not so cool
When you're not at school today, Miss.

Tick-tock, tick-tock
Time is really going slow today
It's not so cool
When you're not at school today, Miss.

Rayyan Nawaab Khan

Remember Me!

I come downstairs
And all I can see
Is my dog and family
Staring at me.

I ask what's wrong,
But they don't answer.
All I can hear is
The words, "Look at her."

Remember me, remember me,
That's what I say.
I know I'm staying
But I don't have to pay.

Look at me, am I insane?
Deep inside, I can feel the pain.

Liliana Fernandes (14)

How Much I Miss School

I miss the sight of the teacher's smiles
Makes my heart jump for miles
I miss the smell of the yummy school dinners
Racing there to be the winners
I miss the touch of hugging my friends
Each one of them are little gems
I miss the sound of the giggles on the yard
After working really hard
I miss the taste of the afternoon snack
And I can't wait to come back!

Maisie Grist (9)

Tiptoe

Carefully and secretly, he tiptoes in with his bag,
Empty, and ready to fill up with swag.
Through the kitchen and through the lounge,
He tiptoes up the stairs without a creaky sound.
Through the hallway and through the door,
Trying not to wake the poor.
Turning left and turning right
He suddenly caught a terrifying fright!
Standing there was a lonely boy,
Holding a knife for a toy.

Eliska Bryning (11)

Hood Of Roses

There he lurks upon the moulds,
He knows what the future holds.
His bloodshot eyes, his jagged teeth,
Under a tree, he hides beneath.
Golden amber eyes glistening in the full moon,
She doesn't know it's not safe past noon.
Blood-curdling howls of doom,
Echo around the forest's gloom.
Then he leaps and within his jaw,
A hood he keeps.
With one snap his jaw closes,
Now there is no hood of roses.

Abbie Berg-Walters

Anxiety

Anxiety...
It is the woods at night.
Never leaves your body, clings on with all its might.
Anxiety...
It leaps into your soul, twists itself around your brain.
Takes hold of all your happy thoughts and throws them down the drain.
Anxiety...
It smells like a burnt down building, smouldering in flames.
All your best memories, that's what it claims.
Anxiety...

Lucy Mehrer (10)

The Smile

The smile you see isn't always true
The sadness I feel is nothing new
My feelings are unnoticed
Because I never show this
The thoughts that go through my head
Feeling like I'm numb and dead
Sometimes I want to scream and shout
But I never let these feelings out
The smile you see is never true
But the sadness I feel is something I'll get through.

Italia Rouse (15)

Life

It has ups and downs,
Smiles and frowns
Sometimes you cry lonely tears
But when with friends there are cheers
Sometimes you make a mistake
With that comes a terrible ache
There will be people who encourage
And those who just discourage
Like a roller coaster it turns
With every turn a lesson to learn
There is always a reason for every season
So smile and carry on
Because this season will soon be gone.

Shifaa Rizwan (13)

Christmas Time

Snowflakes fall,
Children shout,
The winter begins,
Christmas trees are out.

Santa filling his sack with presents,
Families decorating their tree,
Snowball fights begin,
This is 2020 Christmas!

Children asleep,
Reindeer flying,
Santa waking up early,
Dreaming of mince pies.

This is our Christmas,
No adults at work,
Children eager to open their presents,
This is 2020 Christmas!

Eesha Gudka (9)

Mystical Dragon Of Wales

You stand so strong and bold
You are a legend of old
Fire-breathing breath
That would choke your prey to death
A deadly lashing tail that never fails
Your claws as sharp as silver nails
Eyes like fire, as red as blood
Would you be scared of me?
I'm sure you would.
I am a scaled beast from the east,
A warrior of the sky.
What am I?

Joshua James Shaw (14)

Football

F riendlies against PSG and Real Madrid
O nly goal scorer that has thirty goals
O nly two-one
T ackling Cristiano Ronaldo
B alls being kicked everywhere
A mazing overhead kick
L oving the game
L oving scoring goals
E veryone cheering my name
R eaching my goal playing in the Champions League.

Rocco Wickins (6)

FIFA Games

F IFA footballers are running everywhere.
I feel like I am in the game.
F ortnite characters are joining in.
A ll of them are playing against them.

G iants playing FIFA.
A nd the giants are rubbish at FIFA.
M e and my dad like to play FIFA.
E very holiday, having fun.
S uch a great game!

Dylan O'Brien

Slumber Town

Have you ever thought bedtime's boring
Or that you can't wait for the morning?
Then
Maybe be you should come on down
To Slumber Town
I promise there are no nightmares
Just a few funfairs
Plus a
Statue of the great Dream Bean
And seventy-five paintings of the Queen
See, bedtime can be a joy
Whether you're a girl or a boy.

Sahara Iftkhar (10)

The Unseen

At 8pm the claps begin, thanking the NHS for what they are doing.
Lifesavers, food providers, teachers and farmers.
All keyworkers putting others first.
Never to be forgotten in the fight in lifting the curse.
Birds singing, no planes in the sky;
Not seeing my grandparents makes me cry.
The worry inside for what I can't see,
Making the whole world change in the turn of a key.

Amy McWiggan (13)

The Queen

There is an old lady who is 93,
She lives in Windsor Castle and drinks lots of tea.
Her name is Elizabeth, also known as the Queen,
She is the longest-reigning monarch we've ever seen.
She was crowned Queen in June 1963,
Her favourite dogs are her pet corgis.
Her face is on a stamp and on money,
She has two birthdays a year - isn't she lucky!

Zara Hann (9)

A Bomb In My Head!

A bomb in my head!
I think I'm nearly dead
I'm having an outrage now!
Gunpowder in my ear
Fuse coming out at the rear
I'm acting like an old brown cow!
Quick put it out
The spark should be nout
Please somebody help meeeeee!

Flash, bang, fizzle, sizzle!
I need drizzle!
It's really too late!
I think I've reached my fate!
Hopefully, you'll remember me!

Josh Marston

Daring Dad

My dad is very daring
He's also quite caring
We go on trips in the morning
And he never stops yawning
He drinks never-ending amounts of coffee
And stays away from toffee
We do things all the time
Like giving glitter its shine
He's my number one idol
And I'm his, kind of
He is the best dad
Even when he gets mad.

Safiyah Iqbal

Jupiter

Selfish and stingy Jupiter levitates around in the pitch-black sky,
She cloaks herself in darkness as her bulky body screams in terror,
Raging and stomping as she pleases like a queen,
Her ragged, burnt clothes turn into ash and dust as her volcanic storm passes,
Her demonic face and her snooty personality rises to be the largest,
But beyond all that,
She just needs a friend.

Lily-Grace Morrison (9)

Coronavirus

Face masks, gloves, gives me a kick!
Thanks to the COVID-19 pandemic.
Family time, homeschooling, lots of this,
Though still plenty to miss!
Physical touch, non-virtual class, says nobody, "Long may it last"!
It's not all bad though,
Before we all thought we'd go mad, but no.
Face masks, gloves, gives me a kick,
When I think of lockdown, it makes me sick!

Micha Max Goldberg (11)

Thanking My Mum

I thank my mum for all the support,
I thank my mum for all the hugs,
I thank my mum for all the kindness she has given me,
I thank my mum for giving birth to me,
I thank my mum for making me alive,
I thank my mum for making me enjoy,
I thank my mum for making me your little toy,
I thank my mum for inspiring me to be who I am,
I thank my mum for being my inspiring hero.

Malaika Malik (15)

Remember

Remember not to cut down trees,
But instead plant new trees!

Remember not to use motor vehicles,
But instead walk or go on a bike!

Remember not to bully people,
But instead make new friends!

Remember to never snatch,
But instead give!

Remember to never be arrogant,
But instead be kind!

Remember to never stick your tongue out,
But instead give a nice big smile!

Maneesh Pyati (8)

What Kind Of Animal Is That?

An animal with pointy ears, huge eyes and purple teeth.
What kind of animal is that?

At night he goes out looking for tasty treats.
What kind of animal is that?

He eats brains, drinks blood and likes to read.
What kind of animal is that?

It lives in the woods, likes a swim, scares people and loves babies.
What kind of animal is that?
What kind of animal is that?

Kayla Thompson (9)

My Pet Parrot

Mango is a parrot
But she's very noisy
She likes to say 'wash up' and 'go shop'
She rings her bell when something's good
And she likes to eat our food
She is also very messy
And likes to hang upside down
"Coco," she says because that's my dog
Who likes to clear up Mango's mess.

Hannah Key

If I Were A Horse

H ard workers labouring tirelessly every day
O pen senses aware in every single way
R eally clever, sometimes learning something new
S uperb sight, seeing everything that passes by
E xcellent hearing, listening to lots of animals as they go
S ensitive, smelling smells they will probably know.

Bethan Rennie (12)

Out In The Storm

Out in the storm,
I can hear the roaring thunder coming over me.

Out in the storm,
I can feel the heavy rain pouring on me.

Out in the storm,
I can see the noisy hail coming down on me.

Now it's over,
The storm has stopped
But when the floor comes
Don't use a mop.

Karl Armstrong

The Land Of Dinosaurs

Once upon a time, a bush smelt of dinosaur meat,
A dinosaur jumped out of a bush
With a unicorn baby,
Another dinosaur jumped out of the bush,
All of them were friends,
Two dinosaurs were herbivores,
Two baby unicorns were herbivores,
There were two carnivores,
They were all the best of friends.

Taylor Cash (10)

Crazy Hair

There was a girl called Claire,
With black and curly crazy hair!
It was hard to brush,
She couldn't do it in a rush.
It was even worse when she got out of bed,
So she tied it in a ribbon on top of her head.
When she washed it in the shower,
It stuck up like the Eiffel Tower.
Then she shaved her hair,
And her head was very bare.

Lily-May Spence (8)

Lockdown

L uckily my mum is homeschooling me
O verreacting if I get something right
C uddling on the sofa when schoolwork is done
K icking the ball in the house and garden
D ancing to The Beatles
O ver-exercising
W ashing the windows every day
N ap time now!

Jorja Cleall (8)

Stay In And Save Lives

People are acting normal but normal is not what it is
This virus is too big a risk as it is
It takes hold and gives you a cold
And a cough is what it is
So stay at home but not alone
And be the saviour of our lives
Hope you take some of our advice
Stay in and save lives
And save our NHS.

Faith-Rose Ambler (7)

My Thoughts About Xmas And Winter

Winter is here again
Another long year fading away
But still excited for one special day
Just remember
That one day
All the children get to play
And laugh and shout and go bray
Getting presents
And eating roast turkey
That one special day...

It's Christmas again!

Lithumi Nimthara Mahamalage (12)

A Shark On A Cloud

When I looked up,
There was a shark on a cloud,
He was big and very loud,
He was jumping and thumping,
He was singing and thinking
Of what he could eat,
He thought of a rat,
Which was very bad,
He thought of a cloud,
Which he ate,
It was sick,
The shark ate it in bits.

Ishaq Ahmed

The Berlin Wall

I am the symbol of the oppressed
A physical division of a people
Dying to be whole

I watch as those who oppose me
Go under, over, through me
In search of better times

They watch on as I fall
Meeting my demise
From the rubble of my wall, a united nation will rise.

Joe Nolan

Black Lives Matter

It's been too hard living,
But I'm afraid to die.
They say put your hands behind your head,
I start to cry.
I want equality, I need unity,
Yes, we can do this with an opportunity.
We're on a mission,
A great expedition,
To tell the world
Black lives matter.

Jeremiah Powell (11)

My Brother

He picks his nose
He dances about
He has smelly toes
And he likes to pout

He makes a mess
He eats all my snacks
He makes me stress
And he likes to attack

He goes red with anger
He is my bro
He thinks he's Black Panther
And he's my hero.

Max Usher (7)

What Matters

F amily will always be there for you
A ll the time behind your back, help and care
M e and you as a family means so much fun
I f you are sad they will always be there
L ove, joy, happiness is all what family is about
Y ou and me will always be family!

Ela Aslan (9)

Life As Me

Life as me,
I dance,
I kick,
I love,
I hug,
They're all different,
But this is the life of me.

You
Swim,
Party,
Ballet,
All different,
But that is the life of you.

Me and you,
Both different,
Not one shall be the same!

Lainey Mccormack (12)

Dandelion

A dandelion looks like a fluffy cloud
A dandelion sounds like an ice cream
A dandelion smells like a jelly rainbow cake with ice cream
A dandelion feels like jelly dripping down from the sky
A dandelion tastes like a cherry
A dandelion makes me feel happy because it smells like heaven.

Eviee Olivia Piesley (6)

Lockdown Poem

Last day of school was the 19th of March
Miss my friends, football and teachers too
Learning at home is okay
But not as fun as being in school
Stay safe is what we have to do
Until this virus has gone away
So see you all shortly
Hopefully, school will be open again soon.

Daniel Hemmings

Teenage Things

You said I was rough around the edges,
Clouds unfurling away from me like new dimensions,
billowing like smoke.
You made me work on keeping myself so completely in the lines.
There is nothing beautiful about self-destruction,
Yet it seems an inevitable page I'm not allowed to skip.

Amie Ward

The Rainforest

Rainforests are very tall
A beautiful place with lots of green trees
Noisy animals and big long snakes
Howling monkeys, spiders, bugs and even butterflies
I would like to meet
All magical colours, sounds and smells,
I wish I could go to the rainforest for just one day.

Maddison Mitchell (9)

Gloopy Glooper

Slimy slurping,
Giant burping,
Speedy, long,
Stinky pong,
See-through blue,
Yelling, "boo!"
Twenty eyes,
Munches pies,
Spiky hair,
Wears underwear,
Crooked mouth,
Lives down south,
Tiny brain,
What's his name?
Don't you know?
It's Gloopy Glooper,
Champion monster hula hooper!

Declan Prophet (9)

I Love You

For my parents

You are right,
or you are wrong

You are in sight,
or you go far along,

You are high,
or you are low

You are alive,
Or you are dead,

You are far,
Or you are close

But no matter where you are,
I will always be with you
I will always remember you

And most of all,
I will always love you.

Aarvi Gupta

My Grandma

G reat, old, funny memories
R eplaying in my head
A nd I will never forget you
N ow listen
D ear Grandma, Sister, Wife, Mum, Aunty, Great-Grandma,
M ay you unlock the doors of heavens
A nd remember us as we remember you.

Nadiyah Nur Imran (12)

Hour Of Darkness

The trees are hollow, the leaves are light
The stars are glistening in my sight
The Christmas candles glisten and gloom
Fireflies light up my gothic room
The enigmatic shadow follows me
My nerves building up to a pitch of expectancy.

Khalid Ilyas Yusuf (14)

Spring Wishes

I wish I could have fun in the sun,
And I wish I could cycle up the hills,
And walk slowly though the spring daffodils,
And go to the park and play on the swings,
And see my friends and many other things,
When this is all over...

Muhammad Suhayb IBN Ahmed Muhammad (7)

I Can...

I can see the towering trees covering the woodland.
I hear horns coming from far away.
I feel snakes and tigers.
I smell toasted marshmallows coming from twenty-five steps easy.
I taste yummy ice cream from thirty-eight steps north.

Kiruthik Kantharuban (7)

I Want To Be The Sky

I want to be the sky
Because it always changes at night

I want to be the sky because it is always blue

I like the sky
Because it's really far away

I like the sky
Because it's bright sometimes

I like the sky because it makes us breathe.

Leonidas Nomikos (6)

Autumn

A mazing autumn is here!
U mbrellas waving in the air.
T rees are going to sway,
U nder them, the leaves rot away.
M onkeys play with the conkers,
N earby, ducks get cold in the water.

Divyansh Singh (8)

Twins

We are twins
Born as two
People think we're special
But we are just like you
We shared our mummy's tummy
But it doesn't make us the same
We love different things
And to play different games.

Willow-Rose Barron (8)

Rainbow

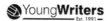

Rainbow, rainbow, it's so bright,
At night it hides,
Rainbow has seven colours bright,
It makes the world look beautiful,
Rainbow, rainbow, makes prayer happier,
Rain and sun brings the rainbow out.

Prayan Patel

All About Winter!

I really like winter because I love warm clothes
I really like winter because I enjoy playing with snow
I really like winter because my mum buys me a new jacket
I really like winter because I like hot food.

Bhavneet Kaur Vigg

Love Letter To A Pea

The pea was perfect, it sparkled in the sun,
Everyone loved it including my tum.

Green and tiny you are so sweet
You and your friends I want to eat.

Pasta, sausages, beans and peas
You're the perfect food for me.

Samuel Rolf (8)

Rhyming Poem - Mum And Me

I was walking in the night,
with a torch which was bright.
I reached home and hugged my teddy tight.
I switched on the light
and found my mum in sight
Then she snuggled me tight.

Vidhya Bomidi (6)

Miraculous Monkey Suzy

My monkey swings like a chimpanzee
It swings on a tree
It is happy
And always energetic
Ooh! Ooh! Ahh! Ahh!
I love my monkey
My miraculous monkey
Suzy.

Lithusha Rasakumaran (6)

Wintertime

The snowflakes are falling in the night sky.
The snow is as white as a feather.
On the trees, there are no leaves
But there are branches.
I can't wait for winter.

Melissa Stoian (8)

Stay Home

Stay home and play,
Stay home and bake,
And do some gardening.

Stay home and dance,
Stay home and read,
To save yourself and the kids.

Maksim Gusakovs

Tiffany

T eddy bear, teddy bear
I s lots of
F un.
F riendly,
A nnoying,
N ice and
Y oung.

Tiffany Ruth Smith (9)

Faces

an earth with no imperfection
grassy windows with small yellow leaves
a diminutive hill, acting as a bridge
a creek with soft edges.

Ava A (15)

This Was Me Today

From the swaying of the trees,
And the tweeting of the birds,
The warm shine of sun,
This was my today.

Harvey Kinch

Young Writers Information

We hope you have enjoyed reading this book – and that you will continue to in the coming years.

If you're a young writer who enjoys reading and creative writing, or the parent of an enthusiastic poet or story writer, do visit our website **www.youngwriters.co.uk**. Here you will find free competitions, workshops and games, as well as recommended reads, a poetry glossary and our blog. There's lots to keep budding writers motivated to write!

If you would like to order further copies of this book, or any of our other titles, then please give us a call or order via your online account.

Young Writers
Remus House
Coltsfoot Drive
Peterborough
PE2 9BF
(01733) 890066
info@youngwriters.co.uk

Join in the conversation!
Tips, news, giveaways and much more!